PHILIP ALLAN
LITERATURE GUIDE
FOR A-LEVEL

TRANSLATIONS
BRIAN FRIEL

Luke McBratney

Series editor: Nicola Onyett

PHILIP ALLAN
UPDATES

WITHDRAWN

Philip Allan Updates, an imprint of Hodder Education, an Hachette UK company, Market Place, Deddington, Oxfordshire OX15 0SE

Orders

Bookpoint Ltd, 130 Milton Park, Abingdon, Oxfordshire OX14 4SB
tel: 01235 827827
fax: 01235 400401
e-mail: education@bookpoint.co.uk
Lines are open 9.00 a.m.–5.00 p.m., Monday to Saturday, with a 24-hour message answering service. You can also order through the Philip Allan Updates website: www.philipallan. co.uk

ISBN 978-1-4441-1986-2

First printed 2010

Impression number 5 4 3 2 1

Year 2014 2013 2012 2011 2010

Printed in Spain

Hachette UK's policy is to use papers that are natural, renewable and recyclable products and made from wood grown in sustainable forests. The logging and manufacturing processes are expected to conform to the environmental regulations of the country of origin.

P01797

Cover images: © RTimages/Fotolia and Sébastien Closs/Fotolia

Contents

Using this guide

Why read this guide?

The purposes of this A-level Literature Guide are to enable you to organise your thoughts and responses to the text, deepen your understanding of key features and aspects and help you to address the particular requirements of examination questions in order to obtain the best possible grade. It will also prove useful to those of you writing a coursework piece on the text as it provides a number of summaries, lists, analyses and references to help with the content and construction of the assignment.

Note that teachers and examiners are seeking above all else evidence of an *informed personal response to the text*. A guide such as this can help you to understand the text and form your own opinions, and it can suggest areas to think about, but it cannot replace your own ideas and responses as an informed and autonomous reader.

The page references in this guide refer to the Faber edition of *Translations* (1981). Where author names are cited after quotations, full references are given in the *Taking it further* section on pp. 92–94.

How to make the most of this guide

You may find it useful to read sections of this guide when you need them, rather than reading it from start to finish. For example, you may find it helpful to read the *Contexts* section before you start reading the text, or to read the *Scene summaries and commentaries* section in conjunction with the text — whether to back up your first reading of it at school or college or to help you revise. The sections relating to the Assessment Objectives will be especially useful in the weeks leading up to the exam.

Key elements

Look at the Context boxes to find interesting facts that are relevant to the text.

Context

Be exam-ready

Broaden your thinking about the text by answering the questions in the **Pause for thought** boxes. These help you to consider your own opinions in order to develop your skills of criticism and analysis.

Pause for **Thought** ‖

Build critical skills

Taking it further boxes suggest poems, films, etc. that provide further background or illuminating parallels to the text.

Taking it **Further** ▶

Where to find out more

Use the **Task** boxes to develop your understanding of the text and test your knowledge of it. Answers for some of the tasks are given online, and do not forget to look online for further self-tests on the text.

Task

Test yourself

Follow up cross references to the **Top ten quotations** (see pp. 88–92), where each quotation is accompanied by a commentary that shows why it is important.

❮ Top ten *quotation*

Know your text

Don't forget to go online: **www.philipallan.co.uk/literatureguidesonline** where you can find additional exam responses, a glossary of literary terms, interactive questions, podcasts and much more.

Synopsis

The play is set in an Irish-speaking (or *Gaeltacht*) village in Donegal in 1833. While all the actors speak English, the audience is made to believe that the Irish characters (who use Irish accents and dialect features) are speaking Irish (also known as Gaelic).

Act One begins just before the evening class in Hugh O'Donnell's hedge-school. Manus, Hugh's elder son, is teaching Sarah, a mute woman, to speak. Jimmy, an old tramp, reads Homer. When more students arrive, we learn that a national school, which will instruct entirely through English, is being established nearby. Maire, Manus's girlfriend, is angry that he did not apply for a job there. When Bridget reports that the 'sweet smell', which heralds potato blight, is in the air, she scorns pessimistic Irish attitudes.

Hugh returns from the christening of Nellie Ruadh's baby and announces that he has accepted the job at the national school, which he will run on hedge-school principles. He tells them about the Royal Engineers, who are surveying in the area and speak no language but English. Maire makes an impassioned defence of the English language.

Owen, Hugh's younger son, returns after a six-year absence. He is working for the army as a translator and he introduces Captain Lancey and Lieutenant Yolland. As Lancey explains the survey, Owen translates. Manus protests that his mistranslations omitted the survey's military implications and that he is allowing the soldiers to call him 'Roland'.

Yolland and Owen carry out their work, disagreeing on place-names. Yolland is dissatisfied; much, he feels, is being lost in translation. Some villagers accept the soldiers, but some are hostile to them; Manus refuses to speak English to Yolland. When Yolland reports hearing music from Maire's house, Owen encourages him to 'drop in'. Yolland is developing a love of Ireland, yet suspects that, as an outsider, he will never be fully accepted in Irish society.

Hugh enters reciting Latin verse. He is on his way to make arrangements for his new job. When Yolland mentions Wordsworth, Hugh dismisses him: he looks to European not English culture. Hugh makes several pronouncements on the Irish language and Irish culture, including that the linguistic richness of Irish compensates for their material hardships. Yolland feels that the survey is taking something away from the Irish.

He and Owen discuss the best new name for 'Tobair Vree'; Yolland insists that 'Roland' retain the name. Owen explodes at being misnamed, but the two soon laugh at the absurdity of the situation.

Manus has been asked to start a hedge-school on an island 50 miles away. He asks to see Maire's widowed mother to discuss wedding plans. When Manus is out of the room, Maire invites Yolland to a dance.

After the dance, Maire and Yolland dash on stage, hand-in-hand. When they realise that they are alone and holding hands, they move apart. Attempts at conversation fail and they move further away. Eventually, Maire picks up clay and says 'Earth'; Yolland responds that her English is perfect. Growing more confident, Maire uses her one line of learned English: 'In Norfolk we besport ourselves around the maypoll.' Yolland becomes excited, and Maire wonders if she has said 'something dirty'. She moves away. In desperation, Yolland pronounces Irish place-names; Maire responds with other place-names. They move closer, tell each other they want to be together 'always', then kiss. Sarah sees them and rushes off to tell Manus.

Owen works, without interest, on the place-names. We learn that Manus saw the couple, but only shouted at Yolland. Manus teaches Sarah as before, but without warmth.

The area is being searched and crops are being destroyed. Maire enters, distraught. She remembers Yolland's last words ('I'll see you yesterday') and how he told her about his village in England — its name and those of the places nearby sounded beautiful to her. She reports that Nellie's baby has died. Lancey arrives, stating that, unless Yolland is found, livestock will be killed, then houses will be levelled. He questions Sarah; she is unable to speak. Hugh and Jimmy return from the baby's wake, drunk. Hugh has been notified that a schoolmaster from Cork has been appointed headmaster of the national school. Jimmy announces his marriage to the goddess Athene.

Hugh lifts the Name-Book and declares, 'We must learn those new names'. It is, he argues, how we remember things, not the facts of the past, that matters. He promises to begin teaching Maire English tomorrow. Jimmy explains the Greek words *exogamein* and *endogamein* (to marry outside and inside the tribe, respectively), and says that if someone marries outside the tribe, both sides get very angry. The play ends with Hugh trying to remember a passage from the *Aeneid* that prophesies the coming of the war-like Romans, who will bring down the might of Carthage.

Task 1

Explore the title, *Translations*. Look up the word 'translation' in some dictionaries and consider its potential meanings. Note that Friel's title is in the plural form.

When you have completed your initial reading or study of the text, name all the kinds of translation that take place in the play. Try to think of translations other than those involving place-names.

Scene summaries and commentaries

Act One

pp. 1–7, from the beginning until *'Maire enters, a strong-minded, strong-bodied woman in her twenties with a head of curly hair.'*

Context

For a son, like Manus, to follow his father into teaching was not uncommon in Ireland at the time. One source of inspiration for the play was Friel's great-grandfather, who was a hedge-schoolmaster. Friel's father also was a teacher and Friel himself taught for ten years. His subject was maths.

Manus is teaching Sarah to speak; Jimmy Jack reads Homer in Greek to himself. When Sarah says her name, she and Manus are delighted. As Manus prepares the room for lessons, Sarah gives him a bunch of flowers. He kisses her forehead, just as his girlfriend, Maire, enters.

Commentary: **Friel's set is both naturalistic and symbolic. The audience might be looking into a real farm building: there are 'stalls' with 'posts and chains — where cows were once milked and bedded' and old 'farming tools' lying around the room. As well as drawing the audience into a believable world, Friel hints at elements of tragedy. This is no rural idyll: everything is 'comfortless and dusty and functional', and (as we shall see in the relationship between Hugh and Manus) this is the home of a dysfunctional family, where there is 'no trace of a woman's hand'. On a symbolic level, the decaying building that houses the hedge-school connotes not only the ramshackle lifestyle of its headteacher, but also a culture in a terminal state of decline.**

The damaged creatures who are struggling to communicate also symbolise this linguistic and cultural decline: the 'lame' Manus is coaxing 'waif-like' Sarah into speech, while the tramp-like Jimmy Jack is lost in the myths of the Classics and oblivious to both the outside world and his own 'filthy' state.

George O'Brien has argued that the opening is 'a vignette that rehearses some of the play's major themes' (G. O'Brien, *Brian Friel*, 1989, p. 103). It is easy to see why. The dynamic power of education is demonstrated as the young woman's first words are articulated and the play opens on an optimistic note. Sarah represents the Irish language and culture, and her successful

attempt to speak — like the celebration of the birth of Nellie's child later in the scene — might symbolise a renaissance for the Irish language. Her first words are an expression of identity and subliminally prepare the audience for that theme, which will be developed notably through the Owen/Roland identities and, of course, through the naming of places, which is the play's main subject. Love, too, is promised. When Sarah presents Manus with flowers, we see a hedge-school version of a schoolgirl crush; and when Maire enters — catching her boyfriend, Manus, in the act of kissing his student — we are prepared for a play in which infidelity will be central to the plot.

The upbeat mood engendered by Sarah's successful speech is augmented by the comic presentation of Jimmy Jack. The absurdity of his choice between three goddesses also allows an equivalence to be drawn between Irish culture and the Classical cultures — as Jimmy says, 'Sure isn't our own Grania a class of a goddess...'. Such humour encourages the audience to feel sympathetic towards the Irish characters; an Irish audience might also feel pride in their culture and the natural, pretension-free manner in which it is enjoyed.

Even at this optimistic early moment, hints of trouble lurk. Jimmy's comic discussion of marriage to a goddess will be reprised in Act Three, when his loneliness and lack of engagement with the real world take on more poignant associations. Sarah's speech will be silenced, and Manus's joyful comment, 'Soon you'll be telling me all the secrets that have been in that head of yours all these years' (p. 3), will be proved prophetic when she tells him what Maire was doing after the dance.

pp. 7–20, from 'She is carrying a small can of milk' to 'Sure the bugger's hardly fit to walk.'

Bridget arrives with Doalty, who brandishes a stolen surveyor's pole. A national school, which will instruct entirely through English, is being set up in the area. Maire is angry that Manus did not apply for a teaching job there. She is getting ready to emigrate to America and is critical of the pessimistic attitudes of the Irish; she is contemptuous of Bridget's report of the 'sweet smell' — a sign of a disease that could ruin the potato crop.

Commentary: **Friel conveys expository details dramatically. Through the mention of the letter that Manus wrote for Biddy Hanna, we discover that a national school is being built, but also**

> **Context**
>
> During the eighteenth century and for the first two decades or so of the nineteenth century, the hedge-school master was an important figure in Irish village life. He would have assisted people with legal matters, he would have been a trusted adviser and he would have written letters for villagers (for which service he would have claimed a fee).

❰ Top ten *quotation*

Task 2

Remind yourself of the dialogue between Maire and Manus as well as the stage directions that show their actions and body language (pp. 7–10).

Re-read and perform this section with your fellow students.

After several readings (and a mini-performance if possible) discuss the subtext: what do you think is going on *underneath* what is actually said?

Comment on the ways in which Friel establishes the character of Maire and presents her relationship with Manus.

hear an alternative view of the hedge-school: that the 'drunken schoolmaster' and his 'lame son' are 'wasting good people's time and money'. We later learn that Hugh's school is losing pupils: Nora Dan has left and Sean Beag is 'at the salmon'. Doalty, the joker, who likes to occupy 'the back seat' of the class, makes merry with a comically phallic surveyor's pole — 'What d'you make of that for an implement, Bridget? Wouldn't that make a great aul shaft for your churn?' — and enjoys recounting his story of moving such poles to confuse the Royal Engineers. On the surface, his action — like a student of today stealing a traffic cone — is a prank, but Friel is also using such comedy to prepare the audience for serious themes. As the more earnest Manus notes, the action was 'a gesture...to indicate a...presence'.

While Doalty and Bridget might represent ordinary Irish young people, Maire represents those more ambitious and receptive to change. On two occasions she makes persuasive speeches that question the prevailing attitudes in Baile Beag (and Ireland as a whole). She stands up for her beliefs in front of the whole class, arguing that English, not Irish, Latin or Greek, should be taught. This challenges the very foundations of Hugh's school and articulates an alternative philosophy of language: while the hedge-school prizes the study of the classics and sees learning as an end in itself, Maire wants to learn English as a means to material improvement. She sets up an opposition in which English is an enabler of progress and Irish is a 'barrier to modern progress'. While she quotes Daniel O'Connell and engages with contemporary debates about the Irish language, her advocacy of English is not just political: it is personal. She needs English to facilitate her move to America. In this way, Friel uses Maire to explore emigration, which was not just a key issue in the 1800s, but also a significant fact of Irish life even in the 1970s and 1980s, as thousands of young people left the economically depressed Republic of Ireland for opportunities overseas.

As well as challenging Irish education and the Irish language, Maire attacks Irish attitudes. Her 'sweet smell' speech rejects victim culture and pessimism, which are almost presented as national character traits. Yet this confident and assured speech is rich in dramatic irony, since the audience will recognise that the disaster, which Maire mocks, does befall Ireland in the next decade, in the form of the Great Famine. Perhaps this undermines her words and might lead some to recoil from her, seeing her as shrill, strident and, ultimately, misguided. Her speech also foreshadows events in the plot, since, after Yolland's disappearance in Act Three, crops are destroyed, evictions are threatened and many seem about to lose their lives.

Friel also foreshadows later events when he introduces another Irish type, the paramilitaries. When asked about the Donnelly twins, Doalty 'shrugs and turns away', then remains vague and reticent when Manus presses him for details. Perhaps on stage the 'silent and alert' atmosphere that descends 'suddenly' after Doalty has begun 'whistling though his teeth' might suggest that Doalty knows more than he is willing to say. The actor's body language and facial expressions, as well as the silence on stage and the shift in mood from the earlier light-hearted banter, might create the sort of atmosphere familiar to audiences of crime thrillers when the name of the chief mobster is mentioned: the kind of silent atmosphere that suggests fear or respect. Such tension sets up expectations that, at a later point, these shadowy figures will have a significant impact on the plot.

pp. 20–25, from 'And immediately Hugh enters' until 'Hugh goes towards the steps.'

Hugh returns from the christening of Nellie's baby. He proudly informs the class that he has accepted the job at the national school, which will be run according to hedge-school principles. He has met Captain Lancey, the officer in charge of the survey in the area, who speaks neither Irish, Latin nor Greek. When Hugh appears to denigrate English, Maire speaks up in favour of the language, which she sees as a passport to progress.

Commentary: **Despite the sinister undertones present through the Donnelly twins, the prevailing mood of the first act is comic. Hugh's entrance is highly entertaining: just after the class — and the audience — have settled after 'the false alarm', Hugh enters, overhearing Doalty announce that 'the bugger's hardly fit to walk'. The humour is heightened when we recognise Hugh's greeting — 'Vesperal salutations to you all' — as the one used by Doalty earlier when he entered the classroom mimicking his master. It would be wrong, however, to see Hugh as simply a figure of fun. Friel's stage directions are ambiguous. He might be 'shabbily dressed', but he has 'residual dignity'; he might have taken 'a large quantity of drink', but 'he is by no means drunk'. He is a 'large man' with a large personality, which we witness straight away through his impressive teaching performance. Dominating the stage, he captures the full attention of his pupils**

Taking it **Further** ➤

Consider how the protagonist is introduced in another play that you have studied. How does he or she make an impact? In what ways is character established through their first entrance? To what extent does the dramatist confirm your first impressions as the play progresses?

Pause for **Thought**

Shakespeare begins none of his tragedies with the tragic hero on stage. Can you think of reasons for this?

Context

There are some reports that drunkenness was common in hedge-school masters. Others maintain that drinking was no worse among teachers than other professionals. We do know that in nineteenth-century Ireland drinking in the countryside was irregular and associated with hospitality and special occasions: alcohol would be offered to visitors and would flow freely at events such as fairs, weddings and wakes.

and peppers his questions and comments with Latin and Greek. He allows the class joker to express his personality, but controls him (when his attention-seeking begins to distract the others) with quick wit, quipping that he was 'appropriately named Doalty' ('dolt' is another word for 'fool').

There is a posturing element to the way in which Hugh recounts the meeting with Lancey. It could be argued that Friel presents him as telling stories in an elaborate language characterised by circumlocution and complex lexis (vocabulary) to elevate himself and his own intellectual and linguistic abilities, yet a closer look might reveal that his lexical choices are actually designed to aid teaching: 'perambulations', 'verecund' and 'acquiesced' all help to reinforce the students' understanding of Latin. He proposes that Irish culture 'and the classical tongues' make 'a happier conjugation' and says that 'English couldn't really express us', yet chooses to ignore Maire's passionate denunciation of the Irish language. Hugh's sense of Irish culture's connectedness to Classical cultures — 'we feel closer to the warm Mediterranean. We tend to overlook your island' — may also be posturing. Indeed, there is a certain absurdity to the presentation of Irish as a cultured language and English as being suited solely 'for the purposes of commerce' — especially when we consider that over 60 per cent of English words have Latin or Greek roots.

pp. 26–37, from 'Owen enters' until the end of the scene

Owen, Hugh's younger son, returns from Dublin, where he is a successful businessman. He is working for the Royal Engineers as a translator. After a warm welcome from the villagers, Owen introduces Lancey and Yolland. When Lancey is unable to explain the nature of the survey effectively, Owen translates his words into language that the villagers can understand.

Owen introduces Maire to Yolland. Manus is angry that Owen's translations glossed the military implications of the survey and is outraged that Owen allows the soldiers to call him by the English-sounding name, 'Roland'.

Commentary: **The mood of the scene is palling a little with Hugh preparing to go to bed and announcing that he is 'weary of' his students, but Friel enlivens it with the surprise entrance of Owen. Friel uses costume to help characterise him: 'he is dressed smartly' and such clothing connotes wealth and contrasts with**

Photostage

Owen's arrival on the scene, in a production of the play at the Hampstead Theatre, London, in 1981

the ragged attire of the others (the stage directions specify that Manus is 'shabby', Hugh is dressed 'shabbily' and that Jimmy's clothes are 'filthy'). Owen exudes charm as he greets each person on stage with warmth and interest. Each greeting is appropriately individualised: the joker receives 'a playful punch', the scholar, a Latin salutation and the 'fresh, young' countrywoman, a big kiss. The ways in which he greets his family members are also telling. He flatters his father, calling him by his full name, Hugh Mor O'Donnell — the 'Mor' being an Irish moniker for 'big' and referring to importance as much as stature. He '*puts his two hands on his father's shoulders*', then embraces him '*warmly and genuinely*'. This reunion with his (probably favourite) son after six years' absence not only reduces him to tears, but almost renders this (usually domineering and loquacious character) almost speechless. By this point the audience will probably be charmed by Owen too. Yet perhaps not everyone is. Manus descends the steps with '*tea and soda bread*' and returns Owen's enthusiastic 'Manus!' with a straightforward, 'You're welcome, Owen.' The younger sibling then '*turns round, arms outstretched*', but Manus's response is not specified by the stage directions.

The subtext might be that while Owen has left, selfishly, for a successful career in Dublin, Manus — as is emphasised by the action of bringing his father's supper — has selflessly stayed at home and looked after their ageing and alcoholic father, allowing his own horizons to narrow accordingly. On stage there might be hints of resentment, even jealousy, from Manus, the virtuous son who watches his prodigal brother return to acclaim and love from the father and the community that he abandoned.

Taking it **Further** ▶

The Christian parable of the prodigal Son is relevant here. Look it up in the Bible (Luke 15: 11–32).

Taking it **Further** ▶

Search the internet for images of *Translations* being performed — for example, the 2007 production at Biltmore Theater, New York, directed by Garry Hynes. Analyse how Owen is dressed. Compare his appearance and costume to that of the other Irish characters and that of the English soldiers. In what ways is he like either group? Comment on how a producer might use costume to present Owen as a 'go-between'.

With this in mind, one might view Owen's behaviour on returning as a politician working a room. Perhaps he isn't so much taking pleasure at being back 'among the best people in Ireland', as charming them in order to make his 'two friends' and their mapping project seem more palatable. Owen even uses 'his father's game' of definitions to introduce the soldiers in a familiar and entertaining way, in which he adopts the role of master, and the others — including his father — take the role of pupils. Just as Hugh did earlier, Owen delights in dominating the stage through his teaching performance, which culminates in his own laughter and applause before he muses on how it is a delight to be among the 'civilised' people of Baile Beag and moves on briskly to business: 'Anyhow — may I bring them in?' If the entire charm offensive has been calculated to mollify the natives, then it has worked, because Hugh, the highest-status Irish character, instantly responds, 'Your friends are our friends' and the stage becomes animated as he directs the others to tidy up. Owen's exit line, which says that his role is 'to translate the quaint, archaic tongue you people persist in speaking into the King's good English', is delivered in a humorous tone. Yet under the sweetness of comedy lies a bitter truth. He fails to mention his initial task — the translation of the place-names — but reveals the longer-term implications of this work: he will be replacing their 'quaint archaic tongue' with a new language, the language of the Empire — 'the King's good English'. This, of course, will strengthen overall British control.

The military nature of the work is also suggested by the entrance of the soldiers. Their red jackets contrast with the drab set, and Lancey's '*crisp*' and formal manner is at odds with the previously relaxed atmosphere. In addition to informing the characters and the audience of the aims of the Ordnance Survey work, Friel uses Lancey's speeches to generate comedy, which some might say serves to mock the English and flatter the Irish. His first public speech is comically simple and delivered in two- to four-word bursts, with repetitions '*as if he were addressing children*'. His next speeches are a comically complex mix of legalese and surveying lexis; they provide a familiar kind of comedy when a long 'foreign' speech is followed by a single-sentence translation.

The comedy, however, conceals the inaccuracy of the translations. Manus has been quiet since the arrival of Owen. He was wary of his brother at first, asking him if he had 'enlisted'. Now he is even more suspicious. The quiet man starts to raise his voice,

Taking it **Further** ➤

Sofia Coppola's film *Lost in Translation* (2003) with Scarlett Johansson and Bill Murray is the story of a jaded actor who goes to Tokyo for a lucrative advertising assignment. At one point Murray's character is given a long sequence of instructions by the Japanese director, which his translator renders as a single English sentence. See part of this scene at the beginning of the trailer on www.youtube.com.

asking tough questions about the translations and exclaiming that the survey is 'a bloody military operation'. He seizes upon Owen's allowing himself to be called 'Roland'. While Owen laughs this off as stemming from an error in pronunciation, Manus seems to see it as a betrayal of his Irish identity.

Act Two, scene one

pp. 38–48, from the beginning until 'You can learn to decode us.'

The scene takes place a few days after the soldiers were first introduced. Yolland and Owen disagree on place-names. Yolland feels that English cannot capture Irish sounds. His Hibernophilia (love of Ireland and things that are Irish) is deepening. While some villagers accept the soldiers, hostility is also evident: Lancey is suspicious of the Donnelly twins; a little girl spat in Yolland's face; and Manus is cold towards him. We learn that Manus lacks sufficient means to marry and that his lameness resulted from an accident — Hugh fell over his cradle when he was a baby.

Yolland reports hearing music from Maire's house; Owen encourages him to 'drop in'. We learn about Yolland's background. He was to be a clerk in India, but became a soldier by chance. Yolland's father was born in 1789, the date of the French Revolution and the dawning of a new age. Yolland says he felt a new era dawning for him when he arrived in Baile Beag; he had moved not just to a place, but into a new state of mind: one that was not 'striving nor agitated', but 'at its ease'. He wants to stay, but knows that part of Irish society will remain closed to him.

Commentary: **As Act Two begins, Friel presents an interesting juxtaposition, which prepares us for the intermingling of identities that is a key motif in this act. Owen sits '*totally engrossed*' at a large blank map, which is perhaps a symbol of conquest; Yolland, '*his eyes closed*', lies, resting his head against a creel, a fishing basket which is perhaps a symbol of the simple rural way of life. It is almost as if they have exchanged identities: Yolland displays the laziness that colonists considered to be to be an Irish trait, while Owen demonstrates the industriousness that is often seen as characteristic of the empire-builder. The characters' actions reinforce this swapping of roles: '*Owen is now doing*' the Anglicising that is '*Yolland's official task*' and Yolland is doing his best to pronounce Irish place-names, which is part of '*Owen's official function*'.**

*Pause for **Thought***

Owen's quip, 'Isn't this a job for the go-between?', might remind us of L. P. Hartley's *The Go-Between*. In this tragic novel a boy acts as an intermediary in an illicit relationship between an engaged female aristocrat and a local farmer. In what ways could Owen be seen as a go-between?

Yolland's jacket will probably have been removed and his sleeves might be rolled up — to suggest the shedding of his British military identity as well as to show him at ease in the late summer sunshine. The *'hot weather'* could also be shown through warmer lighting and the *'bottle of poteen'* and cups lend a relaxed mood. It is important that a production achieves a sense of warmth and optimism at this point, not just because of its appropriateness to the scene, but also because of the need for it to contrast with the coldness and pessimism of Act Three.

Despite the mood of optimism, there are hints of trouble. We are reminded of Yolland's outsider status by the way that Manus refuses to speak English when he enters. By his conceit of using Irish accents and idioms to represent Irish being spoken, Friel allows the audience to understand what Yolland does not — including Manus's antipathy towards him. When Manus declares that 'I understand the Lanceys perfectly but people like you puzzle me', he appears to voice the suspicions of those in Ireland who oppose all forms of Britishness, but Yolland, with his enthusiasm for all things Irish, confounds easy categorisation, defying the stereotype of the British soldier. Manus's entrenched view is the reverse of the one his father puts forward at the end of the play, when he recounts his story of marching to join the 1798 rebellion only to return home without ever going into battle. Manus is not just puzzled by the Hibernophile British soldier's more plural identity; he is troubled by his brother's role in the soldiers' work. His exit line, 'But there are always the Rolands, aren't there?' suggests sarcastically that in assisting the survey, Owen has become a traitor.

The central action of the scene is Owen and Yolland translating the Irish place-names. The way in which the men work underscores their swapped identities. Owen works with alacrity and enthusiasm; his speeches towards the beginning of the scene are longer than Yolland's, keep closely to work-related topics and communicate a passion for his work. For example, he exclaims at the incompetence of previous attempts to Anglicise the names ('God! — Binhone! — wherever they got that') and shouts joyfully when he coins an apt new name ('Bun na hAbhann… Burnfoot! What about Burnfoot?'). Even Yolland is stirred from his indifference to note, 'You're becoming very skilled at this.' Paradoxically, while the Irishman is making the place-names sound English, the Englishman is luxuriating in the Irish sounds. Yolland's developed dreamy passion for Ireland and its language has also emboldened him into defending his dilatory working methods to Lancey: "'I'm sorry, sir", I said, "But certain tasks demand their own tempo. You cannot rename a whole country overnight.'"

While Yolland seems lazy compared to Owen, it is he who comes to the more profound understanding of their task. He says of 'Bun na hAbhann' that they should 'leave it alone' because there's 'no English equivalent for a sound like that' and — later in the scene — he objects to the renaming of 'Tobair Vree', forcing Owen, and the audience, to consider the consequences of translation. Friel uses Yolland to voice his own ideas — ideas that were shaped by reading George Steiner's influential study of translation, *After Babel*. Yolland is presented as one who understands that, in the words of Steiner, 'each act of translation is an endeavour to abolish multiplicity' (G. Steiner, *After Babel*, 1998, p. 246). His arguments about the place-names show his objection to the reductive nature of translation. For example, he values the multiplicity of meaning in 'Tobair Vree', which does not simply signify a specific crossroads, but contains the story of a man named Brian who, 150 years earlier, drowned in a well in a field near the crossroads, while trying to bathe his disfigured face. Friel also uses him to highlight the sinister nature of the enterprise, noting that it is 'an eviction of sorts' and that 'something is being eroded'.

Yolland also recognises the complexities of language and cultural integration. The first half of the scene builds to a climax as he observes that, while he might 'learn the password', the language 'of the tribe will always elude' him. He knows that, far from being a simple model of transmission and reception, language works on complex, cultural levels and that 'the private core will always be...hermetic'. Owen's glib retort that Yolland can 'learn to decode us' perhaps shows that his zeal for the work of translation has blinded him to its implications; linguistic and cultural communications can never be reduced to the simple message of a code. He will see more clearly in Act Three.

pp. 48–52, from *'Hugh emerges from upstairs and descends'* until *'(He leaves.)'*

Hugh enters reciting Latin verse. He is about to seek a reference from the parish priest, then discuss his accommodation requirements with the builders at the national school. Hugh declares that the richness of

Taking it Further ▶

Why not listen to recordings of the place-names, so that you can pronounce them confidently in your readings or performances of the play? You may find the following website useful: http://web.ku.edu/idea/ special/playnames/ translationsirish.mp3

❮ Top ten *quotation*

Irish compensates for material privations and that a culture can become trapped in a particular 'linguistic contour'.

Commentary: **The section of the scene involving Hugh is, from the perspective of language, one of the most interesting in the play. Friel uses Hugh to articulate some of his most profound thoughts on the topic, yet it is unclear to what extent his words should be taken seriously. Perhaps his words after tossing back the poteen are a warning not to expect the truth: 'Anna na mBreag means Anna of the Lies.' Friel's stage direction also notes that** *'as the scene progresses one has the sense that he is deliberately parodying himself'* **and his response to hearing that Yolland lived within three miles of Wordsworth — 'Did he speak of me to you?' — might be more of a joke than a jibe at English culture. Hugh's sense of Irish culture's connectedness to Classical cultures — 'We feel closer to the warm Mediterranean. We tend to overlook your island' — might also be posturing. While Friel might wish to present Irish culture as being rich and vibrant in the first two acts, so that he can achieve greater poignancy when the British begin to destroy it in the third, he does not produce a simple binary opposition in which one culture is celebrated while the other is denigrated.**

Indeed, Hugh undermines our romantic ideas about Irish culture, even if his criticism is sandwiched between false praise:

> A rich language. A rich literature. You'll find, sir, that certain cultures expend on their vocabularies and syntax acquisitive energies and ostentations entirely absent in their material lives. I suppose you could call us a spiritual people.

The first two sentences and the last, it can be argued, are spoken with irony; the fluent central sentence is perhaps more sincere. It highlights not the 'richness' of Irish culture but the poverty of Irish life. He warms to his theme after another draft of 'Lying Anna's poteen':

> Yes, it is a rich language, Lieutenant, full of the mythologies of fantasy and hope and self-deception — a syntax opulent with tomorrows. It is our response to mud cabins and a diet of potatoes; our only method of replying to...inevitabilities.

Again the shortcomings of Irish life emerge, and Hugh's sense of the Irish as a passive people, who are unable to respond to the 'inevitabilities' of a changing world, might remind some of Maire's speech that attacked Irish pessimism. If Friel is

...Friel...does not produce a simple binary opposition in which one culture is celebrated while the other is denigrated

Top ten *quotation* ❯

Top ten *quotation* ❯

suggesting that these are Hugh's true feelings, then perhaps this is why he offered no resistance to Maire in Act One, when she stood up for Daniel O'Connell and the need to embrace English. However, unlike Maire's opinions, Hugh's are presented in poetic, multivalent terms, and, even if they do criticise Irish culture, they do so with a tone of regret.

Hugh's speeches in this act are at the very heart of Friel's exploration of language and the play itself. His exit speech famously uses phrases from George Steiner, but such is Hugh's pompous, didactic tone and so apt are the metaphors from cartography that the lines come convincingly from the mouth of the hedge-school master:

> ...words are signals, counters. They are not immortal. And it can happen — to use an image you'll understand — it can happen that a civilisation can be imprisoned in a linguistic contour which no longer matches the landscape of...fact.

Pause for **Thought**

While some audiences might take Hugh's words to imply that the English language is incapable of matching the facts of Irish life, others feel that for them to be consistent with his previous pronouncements, we have to interpret them as implying that *Irish culture*, if unable to adapt to a changing world, will be imprisoned by its own self-deluding isolation. What do you think?

Do you agree that there is a sense in Act Two, scene one of *Translations* that, if it looks only to the past, the Irish language will be irrelevant to the realities of modern life?

pp. 52–61, from 'An *expeditio* with three purposes' until the end of the scene

Hugh's words strike a chord with Yolland, who senses that 'something is being eroded'. He and Owen discuss the best name for a local crossroads called 'Tobair Vree' (literally, 'Brian's Well' — after a man who once drowned in a well nearby). Yolland insists that 'Roland' retain the name. Owen, who has been growing irritated by being continually misnamed, 'explodes' in anger. Anger soon turns to joy as the two men laugh at the absurdity of the situation.

Manus is delighted to tell them he has been appointed to a well-paid job, teaching in a hedge-school on an island 50 miles away. Maire enters and he tells her the good news. When Manus is upstairs, Maire invites Yolland to a dance. Now a man with prospects, Manus asks to be taken

Taking it **Further**

Read Friel's source, *After Babel*, for more information on the ideas that he puts forward through Hugh (e.g. 'Understanding as Translation', Steiner, 1998, pp. 18–32). Steiner uses the cliché to demonstrate how language can decay: an expression that might have once conveyed meaning in a lively way becomes an empty 'barrier to new feeling'.

to Maire's widowed mother, presumably to propose. Maire decides to stay in the barn for a drink. Yolland, intoxicated, proposes a toast, shouts out place-names and exclaims that the poteen is 'Bloody, bloody, bloody marvellous!'

Commentary: **After Hugh's pronouncements and Owen's long speech on Tobair Vree, the mood shifts. Owen's outburst that *'My name is not Roland!'* brings tension and conflict: the pauses are moments of suspense when the audience wonder about the consequences of this outburst. He has been charming and genial thus far; this is the only time he has expressed anger. Its vehemence will surely be felt as a peak of intensity on stage; its force is conveyed in the script by three exclamations, an italicised sentence and the stage direction that the character *'explodes'*. Owen's minimal responses to Yolland's embarrassment and apologies extend the suspense, until Friel introduces a masterful twist, where a moment of seriousness shifts into one of comedy. After Owen has asserted his name — and his Irishness — to the English soldier, tension is released as they laugh and invent comic names for each other. The speed of the action is reflected by their overlapping lines. Although this section might be considered comic relief after the preceding tension and the earlier academic speeches, it also develops Friel's themes. It shows that names do matter, and that Anglicising Irish names can lead to confrontation; it also foreshadows Owen's re-assertion of an Irish identity in Act Three. Yet it might also suggest that harmonious Anglo-Irish relations are possible. The two characters enjoy coining names like 'Rowen' and 'Oland', which are blends of both Irish and English. At this point in the play, it seems that Irish and British identities are co-existing joyfully. Both the work of the survey and Yolland's desire to embrace Irish culture are commented on comically: the former via the allusions to Adam naming the animals in Genesis and the latter via Yolland's quip, 'I'll decode you yet.'**

Manus's entry might remind some in the audience that things are not so simple, since he refuses, at first, to speak English 'for the benefit of the colonist', but the mood becomes celebratory when Manus reveals that he has been appointed headmaster of a hedge-school on an island called Inis Meadhon. The moment on stage of the three men — one an Irish Nationalist, one a British soldier and the other a go-between — drinking and laughing together might mark the play's most optimistic point. Yet even here the means to collapse such goodwill is close. What will destroy

Pause for *Thought*

Some have claimed that the presentation of the hedge-school and — by extension — Irish culture in Act One is idealised. Friel, however, defended himself against this claim by saying 'this is a complete illusion' (N. Grene, *The Politics of Irish Drama*, 1999, p. 38). To what extent do you agree with Friel's defence?

Owen and Yolland toast Manus on his job, in the New York production of 2007

What will destroy everything…is not politics, or language, but love

everything — the friendships, the naming project and even the whole community — is not politics, or language, but love.

Manus's new job will provide him with the means to marry Maire. Rather than take a second drink, he rushes to tell her the news; at the end of the scene he is eager to talk to Maire's widowed mother, to ask for Maire's hand in marriage. Manus moves off stage as he takes the milk can upstairs. This is the most lively he has been during the entire play: while in Act One he simply came down the steps to greet his brother after a separation of six years, at this point he '*runs up the steps*', asking Maire how she 'will like living on an island' as he goes. His elation has, however, blinded him to the behaviour of his intended. On stage the actor playing Maire might convey a lack of enthusiasm through her stance and body language; she says little to Manus, and her request that he empty and bring back the milk can might be interpreted as a deliberate attempt both to avoid the topic of marriage and to gain an opportunity to speak to Yolland. None of Maire's lines to Manus are expressive (she displays no pleasure in his good news) and indeed her transactional (i.e. businesslike) sentences before his exit suggest that she relates to him more in the role of a milkmaid than a girlfriend.

Friel juxtaposes Maire's indifference to Manus with her interest in Yolland. Once more, Owen, the go-between, is crucial. He reintroduces them and begins to translate. Perhaps becoming aware of their mutual attraction, he attempts to withdraw his

support; when Yolland asks what Maire was saying, he replies: 'Nothing — nothing — nothing.' Alternatively, this might be played for laughs as a point when Owen grows frustrated at having to continue translating. Either way he attempts to engage Maire in a private conversation in Irish that excludes Yolland. But, just as will be the case in the following scene, Yolland's enthusiasm for the language facilitates communication: hearing the name 'Tobair Vree', he gains a foothold in the conversation, and Owen finds himself passing on Maire's invitation to the dance.

Act Two, scene two, pp. 61–67

Maire and Yolland run on stage, together, having just left the dance. They grow self-conscious as they realise they are alone. Their attempts to communicate fail and they move apart. Eventually Maire picks up clay and says 'Earth'. Yolland recognises the word and responds that her English is perfect, then Maire recites her one line of learned English: 'George, in Norfolk we besport ourselves around the maypoll.'

Yolland becomes excited at what he takes to be genuine communication, but Maire wonders if she has said 'something dirty' and moves away. Desperately, Yolland pronounces some of the names of the places he that he and Owen have been translating. Maire responds by saying place-names and moving closer to him. They say more place-names to each other, and move closer until they are holding hands. They tell each other they want to be together 'always', then kiss. Sarah sees them; she rushes off shouting: 'Manus!'

Commentary: **This scene is often considered the play's central scene. Bringing together themes of love, identity and language, it communicates both dramatically and poetically. It is also richly paradoxical and marks the height of hope for Anglo-Irish relations, yet, at the same time, foreshadows tragedy.**

Friel uses proxemics (the positioning of characters and the use of interpersonal space) and pace masterfully. When the lights come up, there is a burst of energy as the characters run on '*hand-in-hand*' to the music of the reel. The shift to quieter music accompanies a shift in pace as they stop at the front of the stage. They speak to each other in a manner that, to the audience, might at first sound as though they are communicating, but closer attention to the statement followed by statement pattern

and the meanings of the sentences, where one does not really follow the sense of the other, reveals a lack of comprehension. Presumably in the noisy party and then during the run across the fields, verbal language was unnecessary, but now as they stand alone, awkwardness at their inability to communicate emerges. A physical distancing accompanies each failed attempt at comprehensible speech. Soon they find themselves '*a long distance from one another.*'

The desperate attempt to communicate begins with Yolland's use of gesture, which shows a simple level of interaction as, for example, he points and says 'Maire and George' and '*Maire nods: Yes-yes-yes.*' Then, when the use of gestures has been exhausted, they communicate through the elements, as Maire makes Yolland understand what she means by 'water', 'fire' and 'earth'. This might suggest that there is a need to communicate and to love that exists at a deep-rooted, elemental level.

Friel allows much of the scene to be played for laughs. The miming phase might have the comedy appeal of a Charlie Chaplin film, while some of the verbal attempts to communicate amuse in a manner reminiscent of Lancey's attempts to talk to the class in Act One, when he adopted '*a staccato style... with equal and absurd emphasis on each word*'. The scene also includes some of the play's funniest lines. For example, after Maire's painful attempt to communicate by picking up '*a handful of clay*', Yolland exclaims, 'Earth! Of course — earth! Earth. Earth. Good Lord, Maire, your English is perfect!' The next laughs are perfectly set up as Friel builds anticipation by having Maire silence Yolland as she tries to remember her one line of English. The fluid, conversational delivery of 'in Norfolk we besport ourselves around the maypoll' is very amusing on stage — especially since the audience also remembers the line from Act One. Friel sustains the comic mood with Yolland's excited reminiscences about Norfolk life, initially thinking that Maire understood what she was saying. The climax of this comic sequence usually gets the loudest laugh of the evening, when Maire misunderstands his enthusiasm provoked by her line and says: 'Mother of God, my Aunt Mary wouldn't have taught me something dirty, would she?'

This line also marks a twist in the scene. When Yolland extends his hand, Maire interprets this as a sexually forward gesture and '*turns away*'. She moves further away with each of Yolland's

...there is a need to communicate and to love that exists at a deep-rooted, elemental level

Task 4

Discuss with your fellow students the reasons why the actors in the National Theatre production of *Translations* in 2005 chose to refer to Act Two, scene two as 'the leap across the ditch scene' rather than simply 'the love scene' (see the *Translations* resource pack on the National Theatre website listed in the *Taking it further* section on p. 94 of this guide).

utterances and it is only the shared language of the place-names that brings them together. Ironically, it is the place-names, which the survey is trying to change, that provide common ground; in a reverse echo of the previous scene, in which Anglicised place-names led to division, here Irish place-names lead to unity.

The action of the two characters gradually coming together is poetic on stage, and the characters' antiphonal speech takes on a spiritual, ritualistic dimension. We witness the numinous power of the names as they facilitate a non-rational, but deeper, form of communication. Perhaps this emotional demonstration of the power of Irish place-names communicates the need to preserve them more persuasively than any of the preceding rational arguments. The kiss marks the climax of this central scene. We see an almost clichéd image of love as, in the centre of a dim and moonlit stage, a couple, who have overcome many obstacles, embrace. For a moment everything seems to symbolise hope, not just for the couple, but also for Anglo-Irish relations: perhaps there can be communication despite the language barrier; perhaps different cultures can co-exist; perhaps love can triumph.

Friel, of course, recognises that things are seldom so simple. The twist that follows turns the whole tenor of the play towards tragedy. The formerly mute Sarah sees her teacher's girlfriend kissing another man. Manus's joyful words from Act One, when he said that Sarah will 'soon be telling [him] all the secrets' in her head, have taken on a cruel, prophetic irony. Yet there are signs that the love was not destined to last. Each of the lovers desires the other for the very aspects of their identity that they are trying to shed: Yolland is in love with the language and culture that Maire is trying to escape; Maire is in love with Yolland's status as a British officer and his potential to offer her a new life elsewhere.

Task 5

Consider the role of Sarah in the play. How successful has Friel been in giving her a motivation to tell Manus? Look back at Act One and analyse the ways in which her love for Manus could be suggested if you were to direct the play.

Task 6

Write the entry that Maire makes in her diary after Act Two, scene two. It might reflect her feelings towards Sarah, Manus and Yolland, as well as her thoughts about language and Irish culture. You should aim to build upon Friel's presentation of Maire and capture aspects of his chosen form, structure and language. To accompany your work, you might wish to write a brief commentary that explains how and where you have tried to reflect the source text.

Act Three

pp. 68–73, from the beginning until 'It doesn't matter. He'll probably turn up.'

Owen works, without interest, on the place-names. He advises Manus to stay to clear his name. We learn that Manus saw the couple, but only shouted at Yolland. Manus teaches Sarah her name, as before, but without warmth; she apologises for what she told him.

Commentary: **Friel creates a dissatisfying, even disturbing, effect by the ways in which he uses a dramatic technique that Richard Kearney calls 'reverse repetition' (*Transitions*, 1988, p. 141) — repeating elements from earlier in the play, but giving each one a twist. For example, Owen works on the Name-Book as in Act Two, but this time 'he has neither concentration nor interest'.**

Theatrical elements, too, add to the sense of impending doom. A producer might add grey or blue lighting and perhaps use sound and projection to create the impression of rain. Friel uses the foul weather to lend an air of pessimism, just as in the previous acts he used sunshine to suggest optimism. Sarah and Owen's actions add to the gloom, creating a mood of nervous anticipation as they 'glance up at the upstairs room'.

When Manus, the source of their anxiety, enters, the dialogue contains reverse repetitions. Owen comments on a place-name, The Murren, but rather than it being a beautiful sound (as Bun na hAbhann was to Yolland in Act Two, scene one) he considers it a 'very unattractive name', and, more importantly, his comments to Manus gain 'No response'. The play has shifted from a scene in which two people of different cultures communicated joyfully and lovingly to a scene in which no one is able to communicate with anyone else. Sarah's attempts to speak to Manus (presumably to express sorrow at the hurt she has caused by her report of seeing Yolland and Maire together) are met with 'no acknowledgement'; Manus is about to leave without communicating his reasons to either the army or the men from the Inis Meadhon hedge-school. Even the memories of Manus's final words to Yolland are riddled with miscommunication: he failed to express his feelings fully and used Irish, which was unintelligible to Yolland, who was only

Task **7**

List some examples of reverse repetition — where an earlier element is repeated with a twist — which occur in this act. Try to include aspects of staging and action as well as dialogue. Explore the effects of this technique and compare your notes with those of your fellow students if possible.

able to say '"Sorry-sorry?" The wrong gesture in the wrong language.'

Just before Manus leaves there is a poignant instance of reverse repetition. As in Act One, he teaches Sarah to speak, but this time he does so *'without warmth or concern for her'*. Her utterances move from fluent sentences to quiet hesitations and, when Manus has gone, she relapses into the mutism from which she suffered at the start of the play. Her final words, 'I'm so sorry, Manus...', are only voiced once Manus has gone — a further instance of failed communication. When Owen asks her of Hugh's whereabouts, she *'mimes rocking a baby'*, just as she did in Act One; but, rather than being at the christening of Nellie's baby, this time Hugh is at its wake. Just as the birth and Sarah's ability to speak symbolised hope for the Irish language, the death and the silencing herald its demise.

pp. 73–84, from *'Bridget and Doalty enter'* until *'He stoops to pick it up — hesitates — leaves it. He goes upstairs.'*

Bridget and Doalty enter noisily, explaining that the whole area is being searched. The Donnelly twins are said to know something about what happened to Yolland.

Maire enters, only to realise she has forgotten the milk. She remembers Yolland's last words: 'I'll see you yesterday'. She reflects on the beauty of the English place-names. Nellie's baby has died.

Lancey enters and announces that, unless Yolland is found, livestock will be killed and houses will be levelled. He questions Sarah aggressively; frightened, she is unable to speak. Bridget thinks she smells potato blight, and army tents burn. Doalty vows to fight.

Commentary: **When Bridget and Doalty burst on stage, it is reminiscent of their entrance in Act One, except they are** *'noisier, more ebullient, more garrulous than ever'*. **The mischievous side of Doalty is still present, but events have taken a more serious turn: the army is razing cornfields and there are hints that the man they are searching for, Lieutenant Yolland, has been assassinated by the Donnelly twins.**

Friel keeps the audience uneasy about Yolland's disappearance — giving partial information, but withholding definite explanations so that curiosity is heightened but never satisfied. With each

new arrival on stage we gain further information, and when Maire enters Friel uses her to heighten the sense of unease. The *'strong-minded, strong-bodied'* young woman *'with a head of curly hair'* from the earlier acts has changed: *'She is bareheaded and wet from the rain; her hair in disarray.'* Her demeanour matches her appearance: *'she is in acute distress, on the verge of being distraught.'* After a bit of small talk, the reason for her anxiety is made plain when *'(She looks around)'* and asks if Owen has 'heard anything?'

While neither character knows anything about the disappearance, Friel communicates a subtle sense of death through Yolland's last words to Maire: 'he tried to speak in Irish — he said, "I'll see you yesterday" — he meant to say "I'll see you tomorrow."' The use of 'yesterday' for 'tomorrow' is a Freudian slip that communicates the deeper truth that, for Yolland, there will be no tomorrow.

Lancey's return marks the nadir of Anglo-Irish relationships in the play. Using reverse repetition, Friel heightens our horror at the proposed reprisals: the earlier humour at Lancey's stiff manner is replaced by fear; the comic translations become chillingly serious; the earlier hospitality twists into hatred. Anti-British feeling swells as Lancey commands the centre of the stage and attacks the women with both verbal and non-verbal language; *'Pointing to Bridget'* and *'Pointing to Sarah'*, he thrusts pointed interrogatives and imperatives: 'Who are you? Name!' Like an invader who will use rape as a weapon of war, he presses Sarah to the point where she offers neither physical nor verbal resistance: *'She closes her mouth. Her head goes down.'* The speech that she acquired in Act One is silenced and Lancey has lived up to his phallic name: the 'bloody ramrod' has forced a defenceless woman into submission, just as the British will force themselves on the community at large.

Now that the complex and likeable Yolland has gone, all we are left with to represent Britain is the imperious Lancey. At this point in the play, therefore, it is easy to view the English as wholly bad and the Irish as wholly good. Many in the audience will enjoy Doalty's line, 'Tell him his whole camp is on fire', and will perhaps be cheering inwardly for the underdogs and willing harm on the villain. Some view Doalty's character symbolically: as a voice for Republicanism in Northern Ireland. Certainly the mention that 'The Donnelly twins know how' to defend themselves against a trained army makes them sound like a

Context

Like translation, interpretation of literary texts is never a neutral act. The reviewer from the IRA newspaper *An Phoblacht* (Republican News) believed that Doalty, who joins the Donnelly twins in violence against the British, is the play's 'central figure' (P. Delaney, *Brian Friel in Conversation*, 2000).

proto-IRA, and Doalty's later line, 'I've damned little to defend but he'll not put me out without a fight', elicits sympathy for the Irish who are not just portrayed as passive victims, but are brave enough to rise against their oppressors.

pp. 84–91, from *'As Owen ascends, Hugh and Jimmy Jack enter'* until the end of the play

Hugh returns from the wake, with Jimmy, drunk. He has been notified that a man from Cork has been appointed headmaster of the national school. Jimmy announces his marriage to the goddess Athene.

Hugh lifts the Name-Book and says, 'We must learn those new names.' He argues that it is the ways in which we remember things, rather than the literal facts, that matter.

Tomorrow he will begin teaching English to Maire; he will not start with 'always', which is a 'silly word'. Jimmy explains the meaning of the Greek words *endogamein* (marrying inside the tribe) and *exogamein* (marrying outside the tribe) and that both peoples grow angry at a marriage 'outside the tribe'.

The play ends with Hugh trying to recall a passage from the *Aeneid* that foretells the coming of the war-like Romans to destroy the city of Carthage.

Top ten **quotation** ❯

Commentary: **The final movement of Act Three adds further complexities, denying the audience a straightforward resolution of the plot or a straightforward message arising from the play's themes. When Hugh and Jimmy return, Friel introduces further elements of miscommunication and instances of reverse repetition, which occur in rapid succession. As in the previous acts, Hugh communicates by means of his definitions game, but this time those he nominates to answer — Maire and Doalty — are not even present; he shouts his tea order to Manus, but he too is absent; Jimmy attempts to speak to Hugh, but Hugh is so lost in his own thoughts that Jimmy has to stand in front of him and hold him by the arms to gain his attention. What preoccupies Hugh is a reversal of a situation in Act One: his failure to secure the post in the national school. This reveals an element of self-delusion in Hugh's character: while perhaps not lying maliciously, his earlier announcements about the post and his accommodation arrangements might be seen as a mixture of exaggeration and wishful thinking. Perhaps Hugh exemplifies one of his own theories: that the Irish language — and, by** extension, Irish culture — is 'full of the mythologies of fantasy and hope and self-deception'.

❰ Top ten *quotation*

Elements of fantasy and self-deception are also demonstrated through Jimmy. Reprising his gesture of Act One, he stands to attention and salutes Athene, but this time the action is not comic, but '*grotesque*'. His fantasy of union with a goddess has developed into delusion as he announces their marriage at Christmas. While Friel exposes the self-deception beneath Hugh's pedantry, he also allows him to retain dignity and good humour, through details such as his comic dismissals of 'The Cork bacon-curer!' By contrast, through Jimmy, Friel shows the pathos behind the comedy: this broken character gains the audience's pity as he talks of his loneliness, then weeps, staggers and collapses into a drunken sleep on the floor.

Hugh uses Jimmy to exemplify a further truth about language: 'it is not the literal past, the "facts" of history, that shape us, but images of the past embodied in language'. Jimmy, gripped by a delusion that he can live in the classical past, exists in a fossilised state. Hugh himself illustrates the alternative approach, where the myth is celebrated, but the less heroic, realistic details of life are acknowledged. The memory of him and Jimmy marching to join the 1798 rebellion is presented as having been glorious, but Hugh understands that the truth is more ambiguous than the heroic memory. For him both the heroic and the real can co-exist — something that Friel emphasises as Hugh's speech concludes with a toast to Jimmy: 'My friend, confusion is not an ignoble condition.'

❰ Top ten *quotation*

Hugh's final speech, which quotes Virgil's *Aeneid*, also communicates a sense of violence. The last words of the play speak of uprisings, 'war' and 'blood', which some might interpret as prophesying a rebellion against British rule. As the lights go down — and perhaps the sound effects suggest the destruction that Lancey's troops are wreaking in retribution for the loss of Yolland — these belligerent, yet resigned, words might imply an understanding, if not an approval, of Republican violence.

The style of the speech is also interesting: the normally assured speaker begins to stumble, forget himself and repeat. It seems that, as the Irish language is about to be lost, the language of this custodian of Irish culture is breaking down. We remember that Hugh has postponed Maire's English lessons until 'After the

Context

Friel believes that in 'some ways the inherited images of 1916, or 1690, control and rule our lives much more profoundly than the historical truth of what happened on those occasions' (P. Delaney (ed.), *Brian Friel in Conversation*, 2000, p. 148). 1916 is the date of the 'Easter Rising', a rebellion celebrated by Nationalists; the battle of the Boyne, a victory celebrated by Unionists, took place in 1690.

Hugh and Jimmy Jack, in the 1981 production at the Hampstead Theatre, London

Photostage

Task 8

In your own words, explain what Hugh means when he says: 'I look at James and three facts occur to me: A — that it is not the literal "facts" of history, that shape us, but images of the past embodied in language. James has ceased to make that discrimination…B — we must never cease renewing those images; because once we do, we fossilise' (p. 88).

funeral', which might be thought of as being literally for Nellie's baby but symbolically for the Irish language.

Despite the dark mood, taken as a whole, Hugh's words and actions suggest a need to compromise. Earlier, he was willing to be part of the British education system by applying to run one of the national schools, and — in contrast to Owen, who repudiates his earlier work for the survey — Hugh accepts the need to use the names and, by extension, the new language.

The ending then is tragic, but it also contains the seeds of hope: Irish culture will not die with the death of the Irish language; it will evolve. The Irish will adopt the language of their oppressors, and, in time, great Irish writers — like Yeats and Joyce, or Heaney and Friel — will use that language in innovative ways to express themselves and their culture. In doing so, they will create some of the finest examples of what is commonly called English literature.

Context

Many great Irish writers are considered part of English literature, including Swift, Sheridan, Beckett, Wilde, Shaw, Yeats, Heaney and Bram Stoker (the writer of *Dracula*). James Joyce remarked, 'The Irish, condemned to express themselves in a language not their own, have stamped on it the mark of their own genius and compete for glory with civilised nations. The result is then called English literature' (D. Kiberd, *Inventing Ireland*,1996, p. 35).

death of the Irish language, Hugh will teach English. Lifting the discarded book, he declares,'We must learn those new names…We must learn to make them our own. We must make them our new home' (p. 88).

❮ Top ten *quotation*

Pause for Thought ⏸	*Pause for Thought* ⏸
Language disintegrates at the end of the play, and although the meaning of Hugh's translation of Virgil is easy to miss as the mood darkens and the lights fade, it is possible to think of the ending as heralding resurrection, rather than insurrection. Rather than seeing Ireland as a tragically ruined Carthage, how far do you think it is possible to view the Irish, and their version of English, as the Rome that rises from the ashes of Troy?	George Steiner quotes philosopher Martin Heidegger as an epigraph to his book *After Babel: Aspects of Language and Translation*. Friel used part of this quotation in the programme notes for the first performance of *Translations*: 'Man acts as if he were the shaper and the master of language, while it is language which remains mistress of man.' Consider what you think this quotation means and how it relates to the play.

Identity

In Ireland, particularly in Northern Ireland, questions of identity are frequent and fraught with tension. Where a person is from is often used as a means to categorise them on religious and political grounds, as is a person's name. Even a trivial action such as filling in a form can assume the gravity of a political declaration; what should the Northern Irish person write in the box marked 'Nationality': 'Irish' or 'British'? It is hardly surprising that for many of the characters in *Translations* identity is a crucial concern. Manus, for example, sees Yolland as a 'colonist' and the survey as a threat to Irish identity. Hearing Owen talk of new place-names, he reads 'standardised' as a euphemism for being 'changed into English'. Recognising that renaming often accompanies possession, he views the British as conquerors masquerading as cartographers: 'it's a bloody military operation, Owen!' His strong Irish identity also means that he is attuned to the subtle erosion of his brother's Irishness: 'And they call you Roland! They both call you Roland!' (p. 36).

An even more committed expression of Irish identity comes from the Donnelly twins, who are prepared to engage in acts of terrorism to defend their Irishness, yet we never see them on stage and thus they make a limited impression on the audience. At the other end of

In Ireland… questions of identity are frequent and fraught with tension

the spectrum is Captain Lancey, whose spear-like name makes him sound both belligerent and aristocratic (a lance was a weapon used by knights). Of all the characters he appears the most one-dimensional and he helps to represent the British as being aloof, colonial and unattractive. While there is a range of characters representing many aspects of Irish identity, only two on stage represent Britishness and, since Yolland spends so much of his time attempting to forge an Irish identity, it could be argued that Lancey is the only real representation of Britishness in the play. As such it is easy to see why some have considered the play anti-British.

Yet Friel seems most interested in characters whose identities are least fixed. During Act Two, identities are at their most fluid. This is obvious not just in Maire and Yolland's love scene, but also when the Englishman and the Irishman almost swap identities. In addition to having the characters invent new names that blend 'Yolland' and 'Owen', Friel demonstrates the mixing of identities both physically and verbally as the characters 'roll about together' and 'their lines overlap'. As a result of accepting a plurality of identity, the play has attained a joyful mood, but while the atmosphere on stage suggests that Anglo-Irish relations can be harmonious when national identities are relaxed, the plot and structure of the play suggest otherwise.

Translations might be viewed as the story of Owen, who assumes numerous identities in the play, including businessman, interpreter, outsider, insider, son, brother, prodigal, friend, apologist, collaborator, traitor and rebel. Indeed, the structure of the play charts the trajectory of his shifting identity. In Act One, like a charming, but cunning politician, he prepares the way for changes in taxation by presenting the survey favourably. His final action in the play is casting the Name-Book aside — a symbolic denunciation of all he has done for the British. When he says 'I know where I live', he aligns himself to his birthplace and repudiates many of his former identities; when he says 'I've got to go. I've got to see Doalty Dan Doalty', he means he is preparing to defend Baile Beag's Irishness and fight against British domination.

Another character who experiments with multiple identities is Hugh. While at first he appears to embody Irish identity — he is, for example, the important community figure who promises to nullify any threat to Irishness posed by the national school by running it himself — by the end of the play he is willing to accept Baile Beag under overt British control by learning the new place-names and beginning to teach English. Many of his most memorable speeches question the wisdom of clinging to an identity that is based on fixed ideas of the past. Unless there is renewal, he seems to suggest, 'we fossilise'. It is tempting to consider

Pause for Thought ⏸

How far do you agree that the moral of Owen's story might be that we should pay closer heed to our given national identity, and that experimenting with other identities will only lead to trouble?

Top ten *quotation* ❯

Hugh's position at the end of the play as being similar to Owen's at the play's centre: one that advocates a relaxation of Irish identity and an accommodation with some elements of Britishness. But not everyone would agree. During interviews Friel himself has seemingly expounded more fixed ideas about identity. He has complained about Irish writers being too accommodating to the English, and that 'apart from Synge, all our dramatists have pitched their voice for English acceptance and recognition' (Delaney, 2000, p. 146). He has argued that Irish writers should be 'distinctive and unique'; in particular, they must not simply pander to English tastes; rather, they should offer representations of themselves, their culture and their identity for themselves.

Love

With all the critical attention on the colonial elements of the play and the extent to which it might be anti-British, it is easy to overlook the fact that at the core of the play is a love story. In some ways this love is generic: there are a great many stories, not least *Romeo and Juliet*, which feature forbidden love between lovers from opposing sides of a conflict. Yet the love story of Yolland and Maire is not simply a sub-plot to *Translations*; it is central to Friel's main plot and thematic concerns. It adds intensity to themes that might have lacked dramatic power had they only been explored by means of 'masculine' theoretical discussions. Engaging for the audience, the relationship builds expectations, provides conflicts and encourages the audience members to care about the characters and hence to form emotional, not just rational, responses to the themes. The success of a play is not determined by the ways in which it addresses academic issues so much as by how it is able to move audiences — by eliciting laughter, gasps and tears.

When Maire meets Yolland, she has already seen Manus kissing Sarah and their first discussion shows her impatience with Manus as well as her interest in the 'sapper fellas' who are going to lend 'a hand' with the harvest. On stage she could be angry with Manus and envious of the attention he was paying Sarah, and the comments about the soldiers could be played to provoke his jealousy in retaliation. Such a reading gains more plausibility when the actress playing Sarah is presented attractively, as she was when played by Morgan Hallet in Garry Hynes's 2006 New York production. Manus and Maire are obviously a couple, but one whose passion seems on the wane. Details such as Manus's paltry prospects and Maire's views on the English language place doubts in the minds of the audience about their compatibility. They appear to be living separate lives and have different plans for the future: there was an

*Pause for **Thought***

'Never trust the teller, trust the tale' is a truism in literary criticism. To what extent might we choose to disregard what Friel has said of his play? Is it fair to give his comments on his work the same status as remarks made by critics?

evening of music in Maire's house the night before which Manus did not attend; and while Maire looks forward to emigration and the new world of America, Manus looks backwards to the old Ireland of the islands and the hedge-schools. Indeed, their first interactions on stage — with Maire's sulkiness and sarcasm coupled with Manus's failure to understand her feelings — make them seem like a bickering married couple.

Thus, when Yolland appears, Maire is ripe for infidelity. While there are few lines between the two, an attraction could be shown on stage as the aspirational Irish milkmaid meets the handsome British officer, tall and impressive in his red uniform and standing out amongst the rags of the peasants congregated in the makeshift schoolroom.

It is interesting to note how much of an active role Owen plays in forming the relationship. For example, in Act Two, he encourages Yolland to 'drop in' to Maire's house and, by translating for them, he helps arrange their date at Tobair Vree. While Owen does grow exasperated at having to translate so much, one reading of his character might be to suggest that his role in the survey runs deeper than to translate place-names. Some see him as a traitor, employed to smooth Anglo-Irish relations and make a complete takeover more palatable. Since a typical way of improving relations between warring nations is

Owen introduces Maire and Yolland, in a 1993 production at the Donmar Warehouse, London; note how his cravat matches Yolland's red coat

through marriage alliances, perhaps Owen's role in bringing together an attractive, opinionated Irishwoman and a Hibernophile British soldier should not strike us as surprising.

On stage, the love triangle is dramatically effective. Elated at the news of his job success, Manus is eager to have his marriage proposal approved by Maire's mother, but all that interests Maire is Yolland. Dramatic irony arises from Manus's ignorance of what is going on right in front of him, and the arrangements for Maire and Yolland's meeting provoke humour — as Owen is repeatedly called on to translate — and excitement as the arrangements must be made speedily (while Manus is upstairs emptying the milk-can). Friel juxtaposes two forms of communication: the failed and the successful. While Maire is indifferent to Manus's words and Manus seemingly blind to her lack of reaction, there is urgency, enthusiasm and — eventually — comprehension in the exchanges between Maire and Yolland.

As Friel presents love in Act Two, scene two through Maire and Yolland's shifting proximity and their antiphonal exchange, the audience is swept along by optimism. There can be real communication between those of different backgrounds; there is room in Ireland for a plurality of identities to co-exist; ultimately, there is hope for Anglo-Irish relations. It is the scene with the most hope and the most humour, but it is also the pivot on which the mood of the play turns. When Sarah, who loves the teacher who helped her find her voice, shouts 'Manus!' she might as well have signed Yolland's death warrant. The audience's hopes for the exogamous couple have crashed into despair, and hope of harmony between Britain and Ireland is more remote than ever. Yet, apart from this dramatic twist, there are signs that the love was not destined to last. Some might argue that their love is presented in rather generic terms: they are 'trembling' with desire and anticipation, Yolland wants to tell Maire 'how beautiful' she is and Maire even uses the clichéd line 'Take me away with you.' This could, of course, be a deliberate choice on Friel's part; he is showing that their love is clichéd and unrealistic, for each lover desires the loved one for the very aspects of their identity that they are trying to shed. Yolland is in love with the language and culture that Maire is trying to escape; Maire is in love with Yolland's status as a British officer and his potential to offer her a new life elsewhere.

*Pause for **Thought***

For some critics, rather than offer hope for Anglo-Irish relations, the play's love scene shows the reverse. As Nicholas Grene argues, the 'pathos in the scene lies in its very brevity, the sense of its ultimate impossibility. Within the colonial context the dream of intermarriage is like the attempt at inter-pretation, a hopeless hope' (Grene, 1999, p. 43). To what extent do you agree?

Context

Yolland's status as a soldier might be part of his attraction for Maire. Maire can be compared not only to the woman in Seamus Heaney's 'Punishment', but also to Molly Bloom in James Joyce's *Ulysses* (1922), who looks back fondly to her time in Gibraltar (under British colonial rule) and recalls her admiration for the redcoats.

Characters

Hugh

Context

The name O'Donnell suggests a typical high-status Gaelic family. Hugh O'Donnell (1572–1602) was Lord of Tirconnel (modern Donegal) and he was immortalised in *The Life of Red Hugh O'Donnell* as an Irish hero. Manus O'Donnell (d. 1563) was Lord of Tirconnel and 'a Gaelic chief with pretensions to statesmanship and scholarship' (S. Connolly, *The Oxford Companion to Irish History*, 2007, p. 424).

Despite having fewer lines than Owen or Manus, Hugh Mor O'Donnell can be considered the play's protagonist. His influence reverberates when he is off stage and he is vitally important to Friel's themes.

Friel's set characterises Hugh on personal and symbolic levels. Details such as the '*comfortless and dusty*' room, which bears '*no trace of a woman's hand*', and the '*broken and forgotten implements*' indicate the ramshackle living conditions of an alcoholic widower who is also the custodian of a dying culture.

At first Hugh seems incompetent and self-important. He is frequently late for his lessons, which waste 'people's good time and money' and are largely performances in which he is the leading actor; he treats his elder son as a servant whose duties include taking his hat and coat, his drinks order and his class. Yet Hugh is also respected, even loved: Bridget and Doalty fear his disapproval; when they anticipate his arrival there is '*a quiet hum of work*'; in Act Three they report with admiration how 'Big Hughie' roared at the British soldiers.

The audience's expectations build as the students await Hugh's arrival. Sarah '*mimes pouring drinks and tossing them back quickly*' and Doalty impersonates the teacher, mocking his pedantry and drunkenness. Accordingly, we might expect a stereotype: a stage-Irishman, a pompous schoolmaster or a comic drunk, but while Friel invokes such stock types, he subverts them as the play progresses.

Hugh is a charismatic presence on stage, and Friel gives him an impressive entrance. As Doalty declares his earlier warning of Hugh's arrival a 'False alarm', the hedge-school master enters like a dandy from a Wilde play (albeit a '*shabbily dressed*' one). Overhearing Doalty's remark about 'the bugger' being 'hardly fit to walk', he responds that, while not being perfectly sober, he is 'adequately *sobrius* to overhear' Doalty's 'quip'. This surprise entrance delights the audience, who are made to wait until Doalty's failed attempt at seven times nine for Hugh's retaliation, which comes when he muses that Sophocles would agree with Doalty: '"To know nothing is the sweetest life."' Yet such wit entertains more than humiliates, and later Hugh shows sensitivity by inviting Doalty to define 'conjugation'. The correct response — '*Conjugo*

— I join together' — repairs the relationship and boosts the pupil's confidence: he is '*so pleased with himself that he prods and winks at Bridget*'. Far from incompetent, Hugh could be played as an inspirational teacher.

Hugh seems to treat English contemptuously. While proficient in the language, he disparages it as being 'plebeian' and suited 'for the purposes of commerce'. Yet Hugh's elaborate idiolect — which contains the fewest number of Hiberno-English words and grammatical features — is the most English-sounding of all of the Irish characters. Friel complicates our response to Hugh's beliefs further in Act Two, scene one, when we are told that '*he is deliberately parodying himself*'. Perhaps Friel is using Hugh ironically, to question idealism, as in: 'we like to think we endure around truths immemorially posited.' The phrase 'we like to think we' qualifies Hugh's pronouncement and suggests doubt about permanent truths in Irish culture, as do his actions at the end of the play, when he agrees to teach English, but refuses to explain the word 'always'.

Hugh articulates many of Friel's most important ideas. The toast to Jimmy — 'confusion is not an ignoble condition' — could be read as Friel's acceptance of ambiguity over absolutes. His parting lines in Act Two, scene one develop another aspect of this thought. They are also enhanced through dramatic action: Hugh '*goes to the door and stops there*' then declares that words 'are not immortal' and that a 'civilisation can be imprisoned in a linguistic contour which no longer matches the landscape of…fact'. Such words (which are taken almost verbatim from George Steiner) use the diction of cartography to counsel against clinging dogmatically to outdated ideas.

In Act Three, Hugh's final speech, delivered from on high at 'the top' of the balcony, has a choric, valedictory quality. His inability to remember the *Aeneid* might be seen as a breakdown: the cultural decay that we detected in Act One has degenerated into complete disintegration; he and his words are breaking just as his language and culture are breaking. But as well as symbolising destruction, this speech voices the virtues of fighting back. Belligerent words like 'war' and 'blood' are repeated as the lights dim, and the audience might interpret the kings 'proud of war' who will come forth for 'Lybia's downfall' as the Republicans who will strike back at the British Empire.

Yet, paradoxically, Hugh's final speeches could be calls for reconciliation. Throughout, he might be played as one who knows more than he says — we remember Yolland called him 'so astute' and believed he understood the implications of the survey from the outset. Hugh's

Context

Hugh can be linked with 'Captain' Jack Boyle in *Juno and the Paycock* (1924), by the celebrated Irish playwright Sean O'Casey (1880–1964). While on one level he resembles a stage-Irishman (a figure of fun for the audience, who appeals to English prejudices about drunken and ineffectual Irish males), Boyle in fact provides an insight into the hardships of life during the Irish Civil War; the discord and breakdown in the Boyle family might be seen to mirror the situation in the country as a whole.

reminiscence about the 1798 rebellion is a warning against political commitment: it evokes nostalgia for his 'infant son' and his late wife, whom he terms a 'goddess'; he elevates what might have seemed a justification of cowardice into a paean to home and family.

Seemingly inflexible at the beginning, Hugh proves to be adaptable at the end. The 'dignity' described in his first stage direction is displayed in abundance from the point when he stops pouring his drink and picks up the Name-Book. This symbolises a shift from escape through alcohol towards a sober acceptance of the inevitable: 'We must learn those new names'. But he does not utter words of surrender; he renders the conquered people in active terms. There will be accommodation — 'We must make them our new home' — but this will lead to ownership of the culture that conquers them: 'We must learn to make them our own.' Perhaps the triumph foretold in the final speech is not a military victory, but the 'quieter' triumph enjoyed by Irish writers who, having adopted the language of their conquerors, were able to transform it into a literature of their own.

Top ten *quotation* ❯

Owen

Owen Hugh Mor O'Donnell has the charisma of the father whose name he shares. In Act One he brings life to the stage at the moment when Hugh complains of fatigue and prepares to go to bed. Friel notes his *'easy and charming'* manner, and his movements and friendly greetings energise the room. With ease he usurps his father's role as the central figure on stage, explaining the survey by means of his father's derivations game, and by the time he is laughing with joy at being back amongst the '"*civilised*" people' of Baile Beag, he has won both their affection and that of the audience.

While there are similarities between Owen and Hugh, Friel contrasts him with his dour brother. His smart dress contrasts with Manus's shabby attire. Manus seems to be the only one on stage who is reluctant to succumb to Owen's charm; instead he raises suspicions about the survey and Owen's participation. A director might choose to bring the sinister side of Owen to the fore and present him as a knowing traitor, who chooses to disregard the objections of Yolland, who grows to understand the complexities of language and the implications of translation. Richard Kearney suggests that Owen arrives at the hedge-school 'like an Indian scout preparing the way for the ensuing cavalry' (Kearney, 1988, p. 135) and that he has adopted 'Roland' consciously as a *nom de guerre* to enable him to protect his real identity from the British.

Despite this, Owen can be played sympathetically as an ambitious and successful young man who becomes embroiled in a situation that he is unable to control. His remorse, his repudiation of the Name-Book and his reversion to a fixed identity can be met by audience sympathy. His personal tragedy is inextricably linked to the wider tragedy of Ireland. Perhaps by having Owen played in this ambiguous way a more complex and emotionally engaging conclusion can be achieved than if we were simply to see him as a traitor who receives his just deserts. His affable presence can be a joy in the theatre and in Act Two, scene one there can be a warmth and camaraderie on stage that touches the audience with hope for Anglo-Irish relations in a way that the non-naturalistic union in the next scene can never quite accomplish.

Task 9

Imagine that after the events of the play, Owen writes a memoir of his time with the Royal Engineers (Colonel Thomas Colby, who was in charge of the Townland Survey of Ireland, wrote one entitled *A Paper Landscape*).

Write an extract from Owen's memoir. You should aim to build upon Friel's presentation of Owen and other characters as well as capture aspects of his chosen form, structure and language. You may wish to produce a brief commentary on your extract.

Context

Friel himself has acknowledged the traitorous dimension to Owen, whom he based on an imperfect reading of the Irish scholar, John O'Donovan, who worked on the Townland Survey of Ireland. Friel, influenced by the political tensions of the time, read into O'Donovan's career 'the actions and perfidy of a quisling' (a traitor/collaborator with an occupying enemy force) and acknowledges that 'O'Donovan appears in the play as a character called Owen' (Grene, 1999, p. 41).

Manus

Manus is the dutiful son who remained at home to look after his widowed father, while his younger brother left to achieve success in Dublin (which, in 1833, was almost a world away from Donegal). Manus's meagre prospects contrast with those of his brother, who reportedly owns 'ten big shops in Dublin'. Hugh, who caused Manus's lameness by drunkenly falling over his cot when he was a baby, treats him like an unpaid servant. When Hugh enters, he hands his hat and stick to Manus *as if to a footman* and his first words are a command — 'a bowl of tea, strong tea, black' — which Manus obeys immediately. On stage such interactions have the air of habitual behaviour, and not once does Manus receive a word of thanks or praise from his father. It is hardly surprising that when Owen returns, to the joy of Hugh, there is an element of resentment, or at least reserve, in Manus's welcome.

The type of nationalism that Manus represents is suspicious of all things British — he sees Yolland only in terms of his colonial function, not as a human being. He has links with the more militant Donnelly twins

and looks to preserve Irish traditions rather than embrace any form of change. He appears to ignore problems rather than deal with them: he fails in his attempt to discuss Maire's proposed emigration and he refuses to apply for the job in the national school. While he might be unwilling to 'go in against' his father, another reason might be that he prefers not to be involved with educational (and cultural) change. It is appropriate that when he does secure a job, it is in an even more remote and unchanged part of the country, the island of Inis Meadhon.

Friel presents a slight development in his character, when in Act Two, scene one the joy of his success causes him to shake hands warmly with Yolland and share a drink with him. He has also become more dynamic and wants to seize the opportunity to marry Maire straight away. This more attractive Manus helps raise the stakes dramatically and in the light of such character development, Maire's infidelity with Yolland seems a much bigger step.

Audience sympathy might also be won because of his devotion to his father and his attentive teaching of Sarah. Ultimately, though, he is presented as being too self-absorbed to take much notice of the feelings of others and fails to notice what Elmer Andrews calls 'Sarah's loyal, tender, potentially redemptive feeling for him' (*The Art of Brian Friel*, 1995, p. 180).

*Pause for **Thought*** ❚❚

'The saddest loser in the play is Manus, the representative of the stubborn, unyielding attitude of traditional Nationalist who will have nothing to do with England' (Andrews, 1995, p. 180). To what extent do you agree with this claim?

Maire

Maire is the play's chief spokesperson for the forces of modernity. She recognises that the birth of the national schools will herald the death of the hedge-schools, and she attacks fatalistic Irish attitudes when Bridget mentions the 'sweet smell' that is thought to be an early sign of potato blight. The longest speech in the play so far, it compels attention with its forceful repetition and hard-hitting exclamatories and interrogatives. Dramatic ironies abound, however, as the audience will almost certainly be reminded of the Great Famine which was to come 12 years later and devastate large swathes of the Irish population. In this way, Friel might be suggesting that turning from traditional wisdom leads to disaster. Drawing on the views of Daniel O'Connell, the celebrated champion of Catholic emancipation, Maire argues passionately for the need to adopt English. Bravely, she stands up for this viewpoint in front of the whole hedge-school, and no one challenges her.

Top ten *quotation* ❭

Her viewpoints and her demeanour make her seem more of a match for Owen than Manus; and it is her impatience with Manus and his lack of ambition as much as her need to contribute to the upbringing of her ten siblings that is the impetus for her move to America. While some might view this '*strong-bodied*' and '*strong-minded*' young woman as attractive and aspirational, others might find her strident, misguided and calculating. Perhaps she allied herself to Manus because he is the most promising and high-status male in the impoverished village and her love for Yolland is also motivated by self-interest; while she shows signs of passion, she is undeniably attracted to his '*gentleman's hands*', his officer status and his ability to take her away from Baile Beag.

It would be difficult to deny, however, that the loss of Yolland has a profound impact on her character. Her bedraggled appearance with '*hair in disarray*' mirrors her state of mind, as she '*is on the verge of being distraught*' and it can be imagined that the actress playing her would do so with a more uncertain voice than the one which delivered, loud, confident and well-formed speeches in the first act. Her actions are less assured too: she has forgotten to put milk in her can, she hesitates several times before exiting and she returns near the end of the play having set out to go somewhere but forgotten where. While her final line is wistful, she retains some of her determination to embrace the future, saying of English, 'I must learn it. I need to learn it.'

Yolland

Through Yolland, Friel enables audiences to see the British colonial spirit in a more favourable light. In Act Two, scene two he talks of his father who was born in the year of the French Revolution and how this gave him drive and his life 'endless and exciting possibilities'. Thus, even though Yolland is far from the 'perfect colonial servant', he can understand something of the colonial mindset, and perhaps the audience will too.

Yolland's character challenges the stereotype of the callous British colonist. Many of the play's most entertaining sequences involve him: from the drunken fun in the aftermath of Owen being called Roland, to the humour of Maire besporting herself around the maypole and the joy of the couple finally coming together in the love scene. Accordingly, he is one of the best-loved characters on stage, which heightens the impact of his disappearance.

His is not, however, simply a comic role. Reverential towards Irish culture, he recognises the sinister implications of the survey, which he almost subverts by retaining Irish names. Through Yolland's savouring of the sounds of Irish names and their magical qualities, Friel is able to encourage a love of Irish in the audience as well as demonstrate some of

*Pause for **Thought***

In his 'Sporadic Diary', Friel wrote:

'23 May 1979

I believe that I am reluctant even to name the characters, maybe because the naming-taming process is what the play is about.'

For what reasons did do you think he settled on each character's name? Consider, for example: Doalty, The Infant Prodigy, Captain Lancey, Owen/ Roland, Mr George Alexander.

his ideas on language: namely, that a neutral translation does not exist; that to translate is to erode; and that to name is to possess.

While many see Yolland's character as encouraging hope for Anglo-Irish relations, others suggest that he does little to mitigate the strength of Anti-British feelings that the play engenders. Indeed, some might see him as the exception that proves the rule. He contrasts with Lancey to the extent that he does not seem part of the British Army at all: he rebukes Maire for calling him 'Lieutenant George', he is *'a soldier by accident'* and his ambition is to settle in Donegal.

Lancey

Lancey seems the most one-dimensional character in the play. He moves from being a figure of fun in the first act to a tyrant (or a kind of pantomime villain) in the last. A stereotype of a British Army officer, he sees the Irish as colonial subjects — *'foreign civilians'* — and his character seems as straightforward and serious as his clear but emotionless words. (For another perspective on how Lancey might be played on stage, see the 'Dramatic presentation of characters' section in *Form, structure and language* on pp. 48–50 of this guide.)

Bridget and Doalty

Context

The first actor to play Doalty, Liam Neeson, is widely known for his roles in films such as *Schindler's List* (1993). Stephen Rea, the co-founder of Field Day and the first actor to play Owen, is famous for his work in films such as *The Crying Game* (1992). In the 1981 National Theatre production of *Translations,* Manus was played by Gabriel Byrne, who later starred in *The Usual Suspects* (1995).

Doalty and Bridget, typical young Irish people, bring a sense of fun to the hedge-school. As the actor Mark Lambert put it, 'those Doalty characters, those people who come bursting in with massive energy. That's very exciting to watch, and exciting to play. They're not self-aware characters. There's a naivety about them' (Coult, 2003, p. 163). Doalty provides verbal humour: for example, through his facetious comments in class and his rhyme about the rabbits growing 'an extra lug' before the 'spuds' will fail in Baile Beag ('Beag' here being pronounced 'bug'). Some of his humour is physical: for example, when he *'gooses Bridget'*. At other times his humour is a mixture of physical and verbal: for example, when he is *'brandishing'* the *'surveyor's pole'* and making the coarse remark to Bridget, 'Wouldn't that make a great aul shaft for your churn?'

Doalty also helps Friel explore Anglo-Irish relations. While he seems to be friendly with the Donnelly twins (who represent Republican terrorism), he might represent a more moderate form of Nationalism: his pranks with the surveying poles offer a mild form of sabotage. Even so there is room for interpretation. For example, we learn that he cut a path around Yolland's tent for him and in Act Two, scene two he might seem friendly when he asks Yolland, 'How are you doing, skipper?' Alternatively, this could be simply a perfunctory remark. His next comment, 'Wasting your time. I don't know a word you're saying', might show division, emphasising the gap between the ordinary Irish people and the British officers.

In Act Three, Bridget and Doalty are portrayed as '*self-consciously noisier, more ebullient, more garrulous than ever*'. Like a schoolboy at the prospect of a playground fight, Doalty is excited by the confrontations between locals and the British, who are 'scattering animals' and destroying crops as they search for Yolland. After Lancey has delivered his ultimatum, it is Doalty who shifts the audience's attention from British oppression to Irish resistance as he '*calmly, almost casually*' says, 'Tell him his whole camp's on fire.' Through Doalty, Friel invites the audience to view the events on stage in a wider context, as Doalty observes that 'When [his] grandfather was a boy they did the same thing.' His next line, which is delivered '*almost dreamily*', might represent the feelings of Nationalists throughout Irish history, who, in the face of British brutality, have been driven to violence: 'I've damned little to defend but he'll not put me out without a fight' (pp. 83–4).

Jimmy Jack

Jimmy Jack seems, at first, a primarily comic character. For example, in the first moments of the play there is the almost slapstick moment of him removing his hat to reveal a bald head, not the 'flaxen hair' of Ulysses, the Greek hero he is reading about. He also compares his tramp-like clothes to the 'vile ragged cloak begrimed with filthy smoke' worn by Ulysses after being charmed by Athene, and there is further visual comedy, when the thought of the Goddess Athene and her sexy 'flashing eyes' rouses him to stand to attention and salute.

As well as entertaining the audience with him, Friel uses Jimmy to create the atmosphere of the hedge-school. He comes to the classes '*partly for the company and partly for the intellectual stimulation*', and through him we appreciate the vibrant love of learning that exists in the hedge-schools — for Jimmy '*the world of the gods and the ancient myths is as real and as immediate as everyday life*'. By establishing this cosy, fun-loving, inclusive atmosphere in Act One, there will be a much greater impact on the audience when it is threatened in Act Three.

In the final act we see Jimmy Jack presented as a more pitiful figure. His standing erect for Athene routine is reprised, but this time '*The*

Context

In performance, it is likely that the actor playing Doalty would accompany his impersonation of Hugh with physical gestures that mimic the master and entertain the hedge-school students.

❰ Top ten *quotation*

Context

Jimmy Jack's spirited defence of the fields is reminiscent of a real political speech made by James Nash, a hedge-school master from Waterford. Speaking in defiance of the enemies of Ireland, he said, 'Let them come on, let them come on; let them draw the sword; and then woe to the conquered! — every potato field shall be a Marathon, and every boreen [lane] a Thermopylae' (P. Dowling, *The Hedge Schools of Ireland*, 1968, p. 94).

Pause for *Thought* ⏸

'Playing Jimmy is a challenging part because the actor has to deal with funny moments without overplaying or turning the role into something of a "comic turn"' (T. Daley and M. Jones, National Theatre resource pack, p. 12). If you were directing *Translations,* how would you direct the actor playing the role of Jimmy Jack?

gesture is grotesque', and he remarks to Hugh that 'Away up in Beann na Gaoithe — you've no idea how lonely it is.' He is also used to exemplify Friel's concerns. For example, through Jimmy, we recognise the need to renew the ways in which we represent our past and ourselves. By having become so attached to the past, he has ceased to function correctly in the present. In Hugh's terms, he has fossilised. Therefore the audience may see Jimmy as symbolising the dangers of failing to adapt to changing political circumstances. His final speech is both comic and serious. On the surface it could be read as an amusing remark about a mortal marrying a goddess, but audiences are likely to see the serious message beneath. Talking about marrying 'outside the tribe' obviously brings to mind thoughts of the play's exogamous couple, especially since the lines are delivered just after *'Jimmy sits beside Maire';* the observation that 'both sides get very angry' implies what we have suspected all along: Yolland has been executed for his relationship with Maire. Yet a third context springs to the minds of those in Friel's target audience, the Irish. Words like 'you don't cross those borders casually' remind Irish people of the border in the northern part of their island and war between their two 'tribes' — two tribes that have been growing more polarised since the onset of the 'Troubles' in 1969. Jimmy's words, therefore, might be taken to voice an uncomfortable message: despite the desires of the few — who might like to cross borders, intermingle and even intermarry — the many will use violence to keep the tribes apart.

Form, structure and language

Form

Friel is clear about the difference between plays and the other forms of writing: the 'poet or novelist produces his book and through it talks directly to his readers. But a playwright requires interpreters. Without actors and without a performance his manuscript is a lifeless literary exercise, a kite without wind, a boat waiting for a tide' (Delaney, 2000, p. 106). While it is harder to appreciate some of the dramatic devices when you study, rather than see the play performed, it is still possible to appreciate many of the theatrical ways in which *Translations* entertains its audience.

Many features of form, structure and language in the play are also explored in other sections of this book, particularly the *Scene summaries and commentaries* (pp. 6–28) and the 'Extended commentary' (pp. 86–88).

Set, costume and sound

The play's single set depicts a '*disused barn or hay-shed or byre*'. While this is a naturalistic representation of the kind of place in which a real hedge-school would have taken place, the producer still has choices when creating this environment. For example, the set might reflect the material poverty of life in Baile Beag through the dilapidated condition of the classroom with its variety of '*broken and forgotten implements*' and crumbling, disused stalls '*where cows were once were milked and bedded.*' The characters' costumes could reinforce this: the women might wear simple — even threadbare — dresses and have shawls, their feet could be bare and the ground on which they walk could be real soil. Such a set might show living conditions for people that are not much more comfortable than those in which we would keep animals. However, rather than suggest an impoverished community, a producer

might use the same elements to create an untidy, '*functional*' set that shows '*no trace of a woman's hand*'. Costumes could still be simple, but need not suggest extreme poverty. The 'shabby' outfits worn by Manus and Hugh, for example, could be the typical clothes of scruffy teachers.

While the set remains the same in all three acts, lighting and sound change the atmosphere for each scene. For example, in Act Three, blue-grey filters on the lights and sound effects of rainfall might be used to create a miserable environment that allows the stage to embody the prevailing mood of the act. While the warm lighting used in Act Two, scene one creates a sunny environment appropriate to Yolland's rose-tinted view of Ireland, the cold lighting of Act Three could expose the poverty of the place, making its state of decay more obvious.

The set is transformed by lighting in Act Two, scene two to represent a '*vaguely "outside" area*'. For this scene the action is non-naturalistic: everything from the use of sound to the way in which the characters speak and move has a symbolic feel. Some productions feature a moon, which bathes the couple in a romantic glow. At first the sound is diegetic (it comes from inside the world of the play) — in this case, from the dance and the Fiddler O'Shea. Friel uses it as a sound bridge between the two scenes: the '*introductory music of the reel*', which was played at the end of Act Two, scene one to suggest the beginning of the dance, continues throughout the blackout and is used in Act Two, scene two to suggest the end of the dance. Thus Friel creates a fluid transition, while allowing time for altering the set and for allowing most of the actors time to move off stage. When the reel '*rises to a crescendo*', Maire and Yolland's entrance acquires a greater impact and the audience is being prepared for a climactic moment (strictly speaking, a crescendo is a progress towards a climax, rather than a climax itself). After their entrance the music becomes non-diegetic: the '*guitar music*' is from outside the world of the play and adds to the emotional impact of this moment. Several theatrical elements are working together, therefore, encouraging the audience to respond to Maire and Yolland as lovers: music plays, they are alone and they hold hands under the light of the moon. As well as suggesting the dreamy quality of falling in love, this non-naturalistic scene might support a reading that considers the potential for a harmonious relationship between the Irish and the British as unrealistic — the stuff of fantasy. The poetic qualities also mean that there is a sharp contrast between this scene and the start of the final act. Unlike the fluid transition between Act Two, scene one and this scene, there is a definite halt at its conclusion; after the interval the audience returns to realism with a jolt.

Task 10

Explore the functions, or the symbolic significance, of props and costumes in the play. You might include Hugh's stick, Doalty's surveyor's pole, the Name-Book, Maire's map of America and Yolland's uniform.

PHILIP ALLAN LITERATURE GUIDE FOR A-LEVEL

Humour

Translations employs a wide repertoire of physical and verbal comedic techniques. Consider, for example, Jimmy Jack describing the 'flaxen hair' of Ulysses, then removing his hat to reveal his bald head; or him comparing the 'vile ragged cloak begrimed with filthy smoke' worn by Ulysses to his own attire and suggesting that he too has been the victim of magic; or when he says that Athene's 'flashing eyes would fair keep a man jigged up constant!' before he *stands to attention and salutes*.

Conflict and tension

Friel also keeps the audience 'on the edge of their seats' by building conflict and tension, and creating suspense. For example, in Act One tension mounts because of the conflict between Maire and Hugh. Maire has been established as a strong character: we have seen her browbeat Manus with sarcasm and silence, and we have witnessed her powerful denunciation of Irish pessimism in her 'sweet smell' speech; we have also noted her interest in the English soldiers and her progressive views. When Hugh enters, he becomes the dominant character on stage: he poses the questions, controls the discussion and gives the orders. His status is also evident in his conversational control and in the size of his speeches — he reports at length, for example, on his meeting with Lancey. Despite his seeming tyrannical, the mood that Hugh creates is enjoyably light-hearted. His precise and stylishly formed multi-clause sentence about Irish culture and the classical tongues making 'a happier conjugation' is interrupted by the shout to Manus for 'a slice of soda bread'. The bathos is heightened by the contrasting volume and tone of each part of the speech. Accent, too, might play a part: the actor might use a precise, even English-sounding, lecturing voice to develop the thought about language and culture, but could deliver the shouted request in gruffer, unmistakeably Irish, tones. The humour continues as Doalty delights in defining 'conjugation', feeling *so pleased with himself that he prods and winks at Bridget*. Yet when Hugh remarks that English 'couldn't really express us' and that Lancey 'acquiesced to [his] logic', tension mounts as we note that Maire refuses to play his game; she does not define 'acquiesced'. What might go unnoticed in a reading of the script is obvious on stage: Maire *turns away impatiently* while Hugh *is unaware of the gesture*. Suspense builds as the focus shifts to Bridget, who conjugates the verb. Unlike Bridget, Maire will acquiesce to neither Hugh's instruction nor his ideas. She addresses him directly, 'Master.' Suspense builds as Hugh says, 'Yes?' The reply that the audience awaits

Context

The play's humour draws on several comic traditions: the physical humour of the tramp using his hat and clothing is reminiscent of the Charlie Chaplin and Buster Keaton characters from silent cinema, as well as those of Samuel Beckett in *Waiting for Godot*; the old man with inappropriate sexual desires is a comedy staple that goes back to Chaucer and beyond.

*Pause for **Thought***

Friel has written that 'theatre is an attempt to create something which will, if only for a brief moment, transport a few fellow travellers on our strange, amusing, perilous journey — a lift, but not, I hope, an uplift' (Coult, 2003, p. 30). How do you respond to this view?

is delayed as she '*gets to her feet uneasily but determinedly*'. The script also notes a '*Pause*'. This builds further anticipation in the audience. The mood has shifted from comedy to seriousness, and the focal character is no longer Hugh, but Maire.

Her determination is presented powerfully as she literally stands up to her master, stating: 'We all should be learning to speak English.' Unlike Doalty's earlier scurrilous remark — 'the bugger's hardly fit to walk' — Maire's criticism is delivered directly and sincerely to the schoolmaster. It has an immediate impact — '*Suddenly several speak together*' — forcing Hugh to restore order with the loud command: '*Silentium!*' As well as being a dramatically tense and exciting moment, the audience is alerted to a key theme of the play: language (and its role in conflict).

While we might expect the 'girl' to be cowed by her teacher's authority and her classmates' disapproval, Friel heightens the drama by overturning our expectations. Growing more assured, Maire rejects Hugh's denunciation of Daniel O'Connell as 'that little Kerry politician', insisting that he is 'the Liberator, Master, as you well know'. In a reversal of roles, it is she who teaches the teacher, stating her point clearly and substantiating it with a well-chosen quotation: 'what he said was this: "The old language is a barrier to modern progress."' With a rhetorical flourish, she declares: 'I don't want Greek. I don't want Latin. I want English.' Manus '*reappears on the platform*' to overhear her intention to leave for 'America as soon as the harvest's all saved.' Thus Friel creates a climax to the first sequence of the play: one that combines several plot-strands — the coming of the national schools, the decline of the hedge-school and the arrival of the English language — in a dramatic and exciting way. Maire's final words have raised the stakes even higher: not only has she opposed her schoolmaster publicly, but she has declared her intention to leave both her boyfriend and her country. The climax is followed by quiet on stage. Hugh has no verbal response; all he can do is produce '*a flask of whisky*' and pour himself a drink.

Dramatic presentation of characters

The confident woman of Act One is absent in Act Three. Maire's disordered costume — '*wet from the rain; her hair in disarray*' — reflects her disordered state of mind. The actor must give a layered performance, showing her '*attempts to appear normal*' while suggesting that she is '*on the verge of being distraught*'. Her '*distress*' is presented physically, not just by her gestures when she realises that she has forgotten the milk, but by the three occasions when she '*looks around the room*' and the

Task 11

An associate director of one production of *Translations* wrote: 'in this oral culture the love of story-telling and the delight in banter means that it is a cruel, quick environment where characters survive on their wits. This element could be heightened, but there is already much potential there' (National Theatre resource pack, pp. 16–17).

Imagine you are the director. Explore the ways in which your production would try to achieve this kind of environment.

time when she '*suddenly drops on her hands and knees*' to trace a map of England on the floor. Friel focuses attention on her as she prepares to leave, then '*stops at the door*'. The importance of her exit line concerning the baby's death is heightened by the '*Silence*' that follows. A silence is longer than a pause: it will feel uncomfortable for the audience, giving them time to consider that what 'didn't last long' is not just Nellie's baby, but the resurgence of the Irish language and the hope for Anglo-Irish relations.

Some productions present the play as an indictment of British involvement in Ireland and Lancey can be made into a stereotype. Without Yolland on stage in Act Three, Lancey is the sole representative of British rule and can be seen to show its worst aspects. He emerges as a hate-figure as he marches on stage, his splendid red coat contrasting with the rags and bare feet that the women characters have in many productions. It might also remind some audience members of the red berets worn by the Parachute Regiment soldiers who killed 13 protesters on Bloody Sunday in 1972.

Yet there are other ways to play the character. Tom Daley, associate director of the National Theatre's 2005 production, wondered if the actor could convey 'compassion for the innocent people whose community he threatens to destroy'. In that production Simon Coates's Lancey was unimposing: he was bald and squat and carried his hat awkwardly. The

…what 'didn't last long' is not just Nellie's baby, but the resurgence of the Irish language and the hope for Anglo-Irish relations

Owen introduces Lancey, in the 2005 National Theatre production

John Haynes

script allows such a reading; Friel describes 'the cartographer' as 'small' and 'uneasy with people'. Therefore, in Act Three, he might be played not as a tyrant imposing iron discipline, but as a man who has lost control. Like a teacher struggling to control a class, he fails to identify the real troublemakers and disciplines those who offer least resistance. He could be made to look foolish on stage as he points aggressively at Bridget, then Sarah before he *rushes to the window* at the bidding of Doalty, the class joker. His exit line emphasises his lack of authority: he resorts to the weak teacher's ploy of empty threats, warning 'I'll remember you, Mr Doalty' and saying 'You carry a big responsibility in all this' to Owen. By presenting Lancey as someone struggling to do a difficult job under difficult conditions — as Yolland said in Act Two, 'London screams at Lancey, and Lancey screams at me' — a production might convey some sense of the wider complexities of Anglo-Irish relations.

Perhaps someone closer to home fulfils the function of villain. When Owen returns, his charm offensive could be presented as a ploy to prepare the villagers for the British takeover. Manus shouts at both his brother's mistranslations and his Anglicised name. Owen laughs this off, saying, 'It's the same me, isn't it?' but when Manus replies, 'Indeed it is, it's the same Owen', the actor might deliver the line with irony, implying that the brother who abandoned his responsibilities six years ago is as treacherous as ever.

Treachery of another sort might be present on stage in Owen's role as 'go-between'. For example, he introduces his brother's girlfriend to a British officer, transforming Maire's neutral message — 'Has he anything to say?' — into the provocative 'She says she's dying to hear you'. Owen's role as traitor might also be suggested subtly through costume: in the 2007 New York production by Garry Hynes, he wore a long dark-red coat that was reminiscent of the soldiers' military jackets.

Structure

Chronology

The events of *Translations* take place during the course of several days in 'late August 1833'. Friel uses chronology to create dramatic effects. By setting Act Two 'a few days later' than Act One, he creates the impression that the relationships which were established (notably between Yolland and the Irish) in the first act have developed and that the characters' lives have settled into a routine. Act Two, scene two takes place on '*The following night*' after Act Two, scene one: the jump in time is brief enough to sustain momentum and continue the sense of closeness between the Irish and the British, but is long enough for Friel to bypass the events of the dance and focus on the most important part — when Maire and Yolland are alone together.

Act Three begins soon after Act Two, scene two — '*The following evening*' — but this slight shift in time marks a major shift in mood. After entertaining the audience by relieving tension through comedy and by delighting them with the couple finally overcoming many obstacles to be together, the plot turns to deliver an exciting climax (as Sarah runs off to tell Manus of Maire's infidelity). The audience will leave the auditorium and go off to the interval wondering about the consequences of Sarah's actions. When they return, the mood of joy and optimism has been abruptly replaced by pessimism and dread. Indeed, Act Two, scene two functions as a pivot on which the whole play turns: once we reach the zenith of hope for Anglo-Irish relations, the rest of the play swings rapidly towards the nadir.

Plot structure

The play's three-act structure is, in many ways, conventional. Act One is concerned with **exposition**: the audience gets to know the characters and the situation. Toward the end of this act there is a **disruption** (or a catalytic moment) when Owen and the Royal Engineers arrive, which heralds major changes to the characters' lives, setting up conflicts and complications. Act Two is concerned with the **development of the problem**: the relationship between Maire and Yolland grows, as does the recognition that '*something is being eroded*' by the survey. Act Three contains the play's **climax** when Lancey announces the destruction of Baile Beag; the **resolution** is when Hugh decides that the Irish must make the place-names their own and the audience ponders the consequences of the British takeover.

The play is unconventional in the way its final act strikes such a discordant note. The relative uniformity of mood and the ways in which the act builds tension without releasing it — we feel dread as we ask what happened to Yolland, but the answer is never revealed explicitly — mean that the play feels unbalanced. The resolution, with its open ending, also produces feelings of dissatisfaction. Yet, perhaps this is appropriate to Friel's subject matter. In 1980 the situation in Ireland was

> **Pause for *Thought***
>
> In a review published in the *Guardian* in 1993, Michael Billington argued that 'Maire, the farm girl, [is] as much swayed by a romantic vision of England as her soldier-lover is by the mysterious otherness of Ireland. Maybe the tenacity of the myth is what this fascinating play is finally about.' To what extent do you agree with these views?

> The play is unconventional in the way its final act strikes such a discordant note

highly complex; many were losing their lives as a result of the conflict and no obvious solution was in sight. To have offered a satisfyingly closed ending in which all questions raised were answered might, therefore, have been ill-advised.

The play is also unconventional by the ways in which Act Two, scene two is different from the rest of the play. We have mentioned its non-naturalistic style and the way it takes place in a 'new' location: Friel's stage directions say that '*it would be preferable to lose — by lighting — as much of the schoolroom as possible, and to play the scene down front in a vaguely "outside" area*'. By this location shift, Friel breaks one of the 'three unities'. He, largely speaking, conforms to the other two: all of the events of the play are ordered and mutually dependent, and (while not strictly taking place in a single day) they happen in a constrained time period of a few days. Accordingly, the audience can believe in the events; when, however, the 'unity of place' rule is flouted in Act Two, scene two some in the audience might doubt the truth of the events on stage. This scene also seems out of keeping with the other, more realistic, scenes because of its self-contained structure. It is unified by a cyclical effect that brackets it off from the others: at the beginning '*The music rises to a crescendo*' and prepares us for the climax of the kiss, and '*Music to a crescendo*' sounds at the end to prepare us for its consequences.

Tragedy

Some might think of the play as a tragedy. Hugh might be seen as the tragic hero, who is likeable, but flawed, and falls from grace during the course of the play. He seems to fit the role, since he is of higher than normal status — a hedge-school master was an important figure in the community — and he demonstrates **hubris** in the way that he over-confidently expects to retain control over the community's education and culture by being appointed headmaster of the national school. We might argue that there is a sense of **catharsis** at the end of the play as the audience feels pity and fear at the British takeover.

Alternatively, others might question Hugh's role as the hero. Owen has more lines and the play's story could be seen as his tragedy. His 'hamartia', or fatal flaw, is that he trusted the British and, as a result, his homeland is being destroyed and he may well lose his life in the struggle to defend it. A further reading is to see the play as the tragedy of the Irish language, which is reborn in Act One, but which dies in Act Three. (For more on language, see the 'The Irish language' section in the *Contexts* chapter of this guide (p. 71).

Foreshadowing

There are a number of ways in which future events are predicted in the play. The opening sequence, where Manus teaches Sarah to speak, announces the main themes of language (and translation), identity (and naming) and love. When Manus says, 'Come on, Sarah. This is our secret' and 'Soon you'll be telling me all the secrets that have been in that head of yours all these years', these sentiments are ironic, because the secret that she will reveal after having seen Yolland and Maire together will not only destroy Manus's relationship with Maire, but will precipitate the destruction of normal life in Baile Beag. The idea of secrets and one person being admitted into the confidence of another also foreshadows a crucial observation that Yolland makes in Act Two: that 'The private core will always be...hermetic'. There will always be a part of Irish culture that the outsider will not be able to penetrate, just as there will always be a level of meaning that is lost in every act of translation.

❮ Top ten *quotation*

Many of the elements from Act One are repeated in Act Three, but each one is given a disturbing reversal: we have news of a death, not a birth; Sarah, who spoke in Acts One and Two, reverts to mutism; Owen's translations for Lancey are no longer comical, but serious; Jimmy Jack's comic turn is not amusing but grotesque. The cumulative effect of these reverse repetitions is to build a mood of pessimism and foreboding, which accompanies the audience's suspicions that Yolland has been killed and their fears that the townland is on the brink of destruction.

Contrasts

While Act Three as a whole has a depressed mood, Friel enlivens the stage at times to offer light relief, before plunging the audience to greater depths of despair. For example, when Bridget and Doalty, who '*are brimming over with excitement and gossip and brio*', enter the mood lifts and the pace quickens as they eagerly recount the soldiers' actions and the responses from the locals. There are ten exclamatory sentences in as many lines and the excitement contrasts sharply with the gloom of the previous moments, when Sarah wept and Manus addressed her '*as he did in Act One but...without warmth or concern*'. Comedy arises from the story of Barney Petey shouting, 'You hoors you! Get out of my corn, you hoors you!' and the Classics-influenced exclamations of Hugh and Jimmy Jack. Despite elevating the mood in this way, Friel is also able to make a contrast with Act One: when Doalty and Bridget entered then, a sense of fun and humour was generated by the story of Doalty's prank and his use of the surveyor's pole as a comic prop; now there is a '*noisier, more*

ebullient' — possibly more loutish — side to their behaviour and the humour arises from serious incidents such as the rough treatment meted out to the Donegal countryside during the search for Yolland, which foreshadows worse repercussions to come.

In the final section of the act, Friel contrasts the frantic activity of Doalty and Owen preparing for resistance with the more sedate pace of the drunken Hugh and Jimmy. As before, Friel uses comedy to lift the mood of the audience before dropping them into further despair, which culminates with Hugh's dark and ominous speech about the fall of Carthage at the hands of Rome. As with the Bridget and Doalty's entrance earlier, the humour that temporarily lifts the mood is spiked with bitterness: Hugh lampoons Master Bartley Timlin, 'the Cork bacon-curer!'; Jimmy's comical comments about marrying Athene are tinged with pathos and they acquire a chilling pertinence to the union of Maire and Yolland as he explains how 'both sides get very angry'.

Language

Friel's conceit of using one language to represent another could sound contrived (such as when Nazi soldiers speak 'German' by using German-accented English in some films), but part of Friel's skill is that he gives each character an individualised speaking style. For example, Doalty uses utterances like: 'Shut up ya aul eejit, you!' and calls Jimmy Jack 'too lazy be Jasus to wash himself'. The Hiberno-English usages will be recognised and enjoyed by the Irish audience: dialect words such as 'eejit' for 'idiot' and oaths for emphasis such as 'be Jasus' are in common use, and are often exploited for comedy in popular entertainment such as the sit-com *Father Ted* as well as the dramatic tradition of the stage-Irishman. More sophisticated uses of Hiberno-English as well as references to Irish mythology can be noted in Jimmy Jack's speech. For example, when assessing his choice of goddess, he says:

> **No harm to Helen; and no harm to Artemis; and indeed no harm to our own Grania, Manus. But I think I've got no choice but to go bull-straight for Athene. By God, sir, them flashing eyes would fair keep a man jigged up constant!**
> **(p. 5)**

Common features such as the idiom 'no harm to' (here given a pleasing rhetorical ring by Jimmy's tripartite usage), and Hiberno-English grammar features of 'them' for 'those' and 'fair' as an adverb are evident, as well as features that seem peculiar to Jimmy's personal speaking style (or idiolect) such as 'jigged up'. As well as presenting him as a comic 'dirty old man', Jimmy's language contributes to our sense of a relaxed enjoyment of literature, which is unsullied by any of the pomposity or pedantry that one might associate with a traditional classical education.

By contrast, the English used by Lancey is convoluted, bureaucratic and dull. For example, after having been told to assume the villagers understand him, he explains the survey by saying that:

> **His Majesty's government has ordered the first ever comprehensive survey of this entire country — a general triangulation which will embrace detailed and hydrographic and topographic information and which will be executed to a scale of six inches to the English mile. (p. 33)**

The sentence's complexity, its use of the passive voice, its specialist lexis and its official tone have the effect of distancing Lancey from his audience. It is ironic that this man, who is in charge of the whole translations project, would be unable — even if his words were in their language — to translate the survey's aims into terms that the locals can understand.

The language that Friel gives Lancey also works on a number of other levels: it helps create comedy, since his long and complex circumlocutions are translated by Owen into crisp and simple versions of 'Irish'; it might also be taken as evidence for the survey's imperialist intentions: he acts on the orders of 'His Majesty's government' which controls everything — even miles are 'English'. Yet the real survey lacked military powers and statements such as 'Ireland is privileged. No such survey is being undertaken in England' and that the survey will 'advance the interests of Ireland' are historically accurate. So Lancey's use of language could present him as a bumbling officer, rather than a would-be conqueror.

It is also interesting to consider him in the classroom setting of the hedge-school: he might be made to resemble a new, but ineffective teacher, who at first addresses the class *'as if he were addressing children'*, then, after his words are met by *'sniggers'*, adopts an inappropriately complex style. Owen, who was an effective teacher earlier when he adopted *'his father's game'*, rescues Lancey by expressing his message in a way that is more accessible and appealing to the class.

If at times there seems to be a binary opposition between English and Irish, a closer look at the presentation of Yolland's language will help us deconstruct it. Yolland's speaking style is the reverse of Lancey's.

Context

See the 'Ordnance Survey' section on p. 67 of this guide for further details of the survey's aims and powers.

Context

In an interview, Friel stressed the separateness of the styles of English spoken in England and in Ireland, as well as the 'foreignness' of English literature to the Irish. He called it 'the literature of a different race' and argued that if 'we assume we have complete access to that literature, we are unfair to it and to ourselves. And we constantly make that assumption because of the common language error' (Delaney, 2000, p. 146).

His tone is often wistful and concerned with emotions rather than practicalities. His speeches are marked by non-fluency features, such as ellipses and repetitions, but rather than making him sound foolish, these can show him to be thoughtful and open to complexities. His 'sorry-sorry?' becomes a kind of catchphrase which, in contrast to his superior officer, attests to his desire to understand and be understood. It is both amusing and endearing to the audience. Friel also ensures that there is a romantic quality to Yolland and a poetic potential in his language. As well as him responding to the beauty of Irish place-names such as 'Bun na hAbhann', we are told that he once lived close to Wordsworth and it is interesting that the place-names of his village are recalled by Maire as 'strange sounds…nice sounds; like Jimmy Jack reciting his Homer'. The language that was dismissed as purely functional, might, paradoxically, be poetic and bear a phonological resemblance to Ancient Greek.

Contexts

Friel's life and works

Early life

Friel was born in 1929 in the village of Killyclogher, near Omagh, Northern Ireland. A telling story for one who would become celebrated for his explorations of translations, naming and identity is his account of being christened 'Bernard': an Anglicised version of the Celtic name, 'Brian', which appears on his birth certificates. In an article in the *Irish Press* in 1962, 'He claims: "I have two birth certificates, one which says my birthday falls on January 9th, another which favours January 10th"' (N. Jones, *A Faber Critical Guide: Brian Friel*, 2000, p. 1).

While Friel's father came from Derry in Northern Ireland, his mother was from Glenties in County Donegal in the Republic of Ireland, where he spent the summers of his childhood. (Glenties is as far as Hugh and Jimmy march on the way to join the United Irishmen in Sligo.) This part of Ireland might be seen to have a kind of dual identity, since, geographically, it is in the northern part of Ireland, in the province of Ulster, while, politically, it is part of the Republic of Ireland. His heritage may well suggest a sensitivity to the ambiguities and pluralities of Irish identity as well as to the question of being Irish and living within a British state.

> #### Context
>
> Place-names are hugely significant in Ireland. The official name of the city from which Friel's father came is 'Londonderry'; the prefix 'London' was added in 1613, during the time when King James was 'planting' prominent English families in Ulster to increase English control. In 1978 the council became 'Derry City Council', but the British government has insisted on keeping 'Londonderry' as the official name of the city itself.
>
> When the Irish Free State was founded in 1922, the names of many places were changed to assert a more Irish identity. For example, the harbour town south of Dublin now called Dun Laoghaire (pronounced Dun Leary) was previously known as Kingstown.

Pause for ***Thought*** ⏸

Whereas almost every Catholic in Ireland will refer to 'Derry' (from the Irish *Doire*, meaning 'place of oaks'), many Protestants prefer 'Londonderry'. Thus what people choose to call the city is often used as a means of asserting religious or political allegiance. Attempting to be unbiased, some referred to it as 'Derry/Londonderry', which led to the nickname 'Stroke City'. How does this affect your interpretation of Friel's play?

Bury College
Millennium LRC

Map of Ireland as it is now, showing the border, counties, and places mentioned in this guide

Although both sets of Friel's grandparents were Irish-speakers and Friel learnt the language at school, English was his first language. His father, a teacher and later headmaster of Culmore National Primary School, imbued Friel with a respect for books and learning; yet neither his paternal grandfather nor his maternal grandmother could read. He might be seen, therefore, as being connected to an academically and socially mobile culture, yet simultaneously as having roots in a pre-literate peasant past. It is noteworthy that, at a peak of his fame and critical acclaim in 1986, he chose to edit and introduce *The Last of the Name*, the memoir of an illiterate Donegal weaver, who had dictated his story to his local schoolmaster.

Education

After moving to Derry, in 1939. Friel completed his school education at St Columb's College, Derry, a boys' boarding school whose alumni include Seamus Heaney, the Nobel prize-winning poet and Seamus Deane, the professor of literature at University College, Dublin. Here Friel learnt Latin as well as Irish. After St Columb's he attended Maynooth Seminary in Co. Kildare to train as a priest, but found this 'an awful experience'. He left after gaining his BA in 1948 to attend St Joseph's College, Belfast, where he trained as a teacher.

He taught mathematics for a decade in and around Derry, during which time he was writing short stories. He married Anne Morrison in 1954.

Early writing

By 1958 Friel's radio plays were being broadcast by BBC Belfast, and in 1960 his first stage play, *A Doubtful Paradise*, was produced by the Group Theatre, Belfast. By this time he was being paid a retainer by the prestigious American magazine, *The New Yorker*, and he gave up teaching to write full time.

After his play *The Blind Mice* was produced in Dublin in 1963, Friel spent six months in Minneapolis, USA, where the director Tyrone Guthrie was establishing a new repertory theatre. From Guthrie, he says that he learned that 'a playwright's first function is to entertain, to have audiences enjoy themselves, to move them emotionally, to make them laugh and cry and gasp and hold their breath and sit on the edge of their seats' (Coult, 2003, p. 30).

First major theatrical success

Friel's next play, *Philadelphia, Here I Come!*, which was staged as part of the 1964 Dublin Theatre Festival, benefited from the lessons learned in Minnesota and became the biggest hit of his career thus far, running for nine months on Broadway in 1966. Like many Friel plays it is set in a place in Donegal called Ballybeg (from the Irish *baile beag*, meaning 'small town') and it features a family named O'Donnell. It depicts a situation that might have been going on in any Irish small town at the time (and, indeed, one that will be familiar to audiences of *Translations* through the character Maire) as its protagonist, Gar O'Donnell, prepares to escape the limited opportunities offered by Ireland through emigration to America. While dealing with emigration — surely an issue

> **Context**
>
> In a 1965 interview Friel said, 'I think I'm a sort of peasant at heart. I'm certainly not "citified" and I never will be. There are certain atmospheres which I find totally alien to me and I'm much more at ease in a rural setting' (Delaney, 2000, p. 37).

> **Context**
>
> Some of Friel's early short stories contain elements that would resurface in plays such as *Translations*. For example, in stories such as 'The Fawn Pup', 'My Father and the Sergeant' and 'The Illusionist', the central relationship is between a father, who is a teacher, and his son. In some of these stories the father's school is under threat of closure.

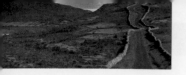

that would resonate with American audiences — the play is grounded in the relationship between Gar and his father, S.B. The play is also interesting formally, since what might have been a typical family drama incorporates an innovative non-naturalistic technique. Friel puts two Gar O'Donnells on stage: Gar Public (who is seen and heard by all) and Gar Private (who voices Gar's thoughts and is seen and heard by the audience alone).

Translations and related plays

Many of the plays that Friel went on to write in the 1970s and 1980s contain aspects that are major concerns of *Translations*. *The Freedom of the City* (1973) is a direct response to the events of 'Bloody Sunday' in 1972. Set in Derry, it centres around three Civil Rights protestors, who flee the rubber bullets and the tear gas used by the army at a demonstration and take refuge in the Mayor's Parlour in the Guildhall (the city hall). The play contains characters who reflect on these events, including a reporter, an American sociologist and a balladeer, and it questions whether it is possible to find the 'truth' in the past. The search for truth and the impossibility of accurately recalling past events is also one of the main themes of *Faith Healer* (1979), which comprises monologues from three characters, each of whom provides a different account of the life and times of Frank Hardy, the titular faith healer.

After *Translations*, Friel wrote *The Communication Cord* (1982), a farce, which parodies characters and situations from the earlier play. *Making History* (1988) returns to more serious territory by dramatising the life of Hugh O'Neill, the Earl of Tyrone and leader of Gaelic Ireland, focusing mainly on events just before and just after the Irish were defeated at the battle of Kinsale in 1601. In a way that is reminiscent of *Translations*, the play poses questions about history and truth; ultimately, *Making History* presents history as just another narrative, rather than an accurate recording of events.

Taking it **Further** ▶

Like *Translations*, Friel's *Making History* (1988) is concerned with language, identity and history. The use of 'Making' in the title perhaps suggests that history is closer to fabrication than fact. At the play's heart is also an exogamous relationship.

Why not read *Making History* and compare the ways in which Friel's concerns are presented in this play and *Translations*?

Later career

In 1987 Friel was appointed to sit in the Irish Senate and in 1989 the BBC devoted a six-play season to Friel — the first time a living playwright has received this honour. In the 1990s Friel's work moved from the larger canvas of historical and political events towards more personal and familial concerns. One of his best-loved plays, *Dancing at Lughnasa* (1993), draws on memories of his aunts in Glenties, Co. Donegal. The play won many prizes, including The New York Critics' Circle Award for Best Play in 1992. Friel has carried on producing popular and critically acclaimed work and is often referred to as 'Ireland's greatest living playwright', although some, notably Peter Fallon, go further and see him as 'the greatest living playwright'.

Historical context

While set in 1833, *Translations* alludes to several aspects of Irish life and events in Irish history.

English authority in Ireland

In 1155, Adrian IV, the only English pope, proclaimed King Henry II's right to conquer Ireland for the purpose of church reform. Many suspect that this proclamation was made after pressure from the archbishop of Canterbury. An expedition to Ireland began in 1171, but until Tudor times English sovereignty was mostly confined to Dublin and the nearby counties. This area of English authority was later termed the Pale; the rest of Ireland remained under the control of local lords. Between the late twelfth century and 1603, the family who ruled the area known as Tir Conaill or Tirconnell (which encompasses what is now called Donegal), independent of British rule, was the O Domhnaill or O'Donnell family.

In 1534 the Tudor conquest began, and a succession of lord deputies ruled Ireland on the British monarch's behalf. The areas of English control grew as they employed draconian tactics such as 'the establishment of garrisons followed by the spoliation of the people, their crops, and their livestock, bringing starvation and eventual submission' (Connolly, 2007, p. 584).

The 1798 rebellion

As exemplified by Hugh's misty-eyed moment near the end of the play, uprisings against the British loom large in the Irish imagination, even if the ways in which they are remembered are not always congruent with the historical facts. When Hugh talks of '1798. Going into battle', he remembers his part in the famous United Irishmen's rebellion. The United Irishmen were made up of both Protestants and Catholics who

---

Context

The word 'pale' originally denoted a wooden stake, which was driven into the ground as part of a fence. Accordingly, 'pale' soon became a term for a fenced-in area, or a zone of safety. The expression 'beyond the pale' came later and means to go beyond the normal boundaries of acceptability.

Task 12

Remind yourself of Captain Lancey's tactics after the disappearance of Yolland in Act Three. Analyse the ways in which they are reminiscent of the real-life terror tactics used by the British to suppress the Irish.

wanted parliamentary reform and the removal of British authority from Ireland. Partly inspired by the French Revolution of 1789 (to which Yolland in *Translations* looks as the turning point in world history and the event which gave his father his spirit of adventure), the United Irishmen's insurrection had four main uprisings in different parts of the country. A total of 30,000 lives were lost in what turned out to be the bloodiest episode in Irish history since the 1600s.

In the light of such events, the English sought to strengthen their control over Ireland. The Act of Union was two identical statutes passed by the British and Irish governments which created the United Kingdom of Great Britain and Ireland, with effect from 1 January 1801. The size of the country and other factors of its separateness meant that the day-to-day government was carried out not from London, but from Dublin. Central control, however, was becoming increasingly exerted, with state intervention in economic development, public health and education.

Daniel O'Connell (1777–1847)

O'Connell was a towering leader in Irish politics, whose statue stands prominently to this day at the bottom of Dublin's main street, which also bears his name. In the words of J. C. Beckett, 'no other single person has left such an unmistakeable mark on the history of Ireland' (*The Making of Modern Ireland*, 1981, p. 347). Early in his career, he sympathised with the United Irishmen. Sean Connolly, however, notes that 'he expressed…genuine horror, both at the time and later, at the insurrection of 1798' (Connolly, 2007, p. 418). Perhaps O'Connell's major skill was in harnessing public opinion and raising political consciousness in the people, making them demand more say in public affairs. As the most dynamic Catholic leader in the 1820s and 1830s, his role in securing the Catholic Emancipation Act of 1829, which granted rights of political representation and public office-holding, won him the title 'The Liberator' (as used by Maire in Act One). He became Lord Mayor of Dublin in 1841, the first Catholic to hold the office since the reign of James II. While O'Connell came from an Irish-speaking area in rural Kerry, he had been educated for a time in France and espoused progressive ideas. The comments made about him by Maire and Hugh both have an air of historical truth; as the historian Roy Foster notes, he 'dismissed the Irish language robustly as a drawback in the modern world, which earned him the disapproval of later nationalists' (*Modern Ireland 1600–1972*, 1989, p. 300).

Hedge-schools

At first it is easy to dismiss the hedge-school setting, its pupils and its teachers as a romanticised portrait of an Ireland that never was. The atmosphere of friendly banter, the poverty-stricken pupil who is fluent in Latin and Greek, and the impressive, sharp-witted schoolmaster seem to have been invented for their entertainment value rather than their historical accuracy. Yet, on closer inspection, a great many of the elements that Friel uses to create his hedge-school appear to have roots in historical sources.

Hedge-schools were the unlicensed schools which grew up in response to the suppression of education, first under Oliver Cromwell during the 1650s and then under the Penal Laws. While there was some variation in the strictness with which laws proscribing the education of Catholics were enforced, to teach was to risk fining or imprisonment. In *The Hedge Schools of Ireland* (a work Friel read and re-read as ideas for *Translations* took shape) P. J. Dowling notes that an informer could expect a substantial reward for information leading to the conviction of an illegal teacher. Accordingly, teaching was a dangerous profession. The term 'hedge-school' carries this connotation: illegal schools would take place in remote areas, typically under the shelter of a hedge, to shield the schoolmaster and his students from the eyes of passers-by. Often a pupil would act as a sentry and give a warning if strangers approached; if these were suspected informers or officers of the law, teaching was suspended and the class would be resumed the next day in a more remote place. When the laws prohibiting Catholic education were less vigorously enforced, teaching would take place in a cabin or in a barn, such as the one in which Friel sets *Translations*.

The atmosphere of Friel's hedge-school is also in keeping with contemporary accounts. Dowling notes that 'the atmosphere of the Hedge Schools seemed to have been naturally lively and good-humoured' (Dowling, 1968, p. 36). He also draws on the accounts of William Carlton, a Victorian writer who was educated in hedge-schools and was himself, for a time, a hedge-school master. Carlton describes the social dimension of hedge-school life and, according to Dowling, 'does not wish to banish from the schoolroom the school-boy's joke, the occasional bursts of merriment in class or even a little horseplay: "it is an exercise to the mind," [Carlton] asserts, "and he will return to his business with greater vigour and effect"' (Dowling, 1968, p. 46).

Friel's hedge-school pupils are taught in a similar way to those from real hedge-schools. Dowling quotes a contemporary account that notes

<aside>
Context

Legislation strengthened England's grip on Ireland. Catholics were banned from being a judge or a member of parliament and denied the right to buy land. While they were allowed to teach, strict conditions meant no Catholic schools could be built and schools had to be licensed by a Protestant bishop. Accordingly, hedge-schools were illegal until the Catholic Emancipation Act of 1829.
</aside>

Pause for Thought ⏸

Friel is precise about setting his play in August 1833. To what extent does this setting, which is four years after hedge-schools became legal and after the founding of the national schools, affect the ways in which we view the characters and events of the play?

the way in which pupils were taught individually, rather than in groups according to ability. Writing and arithmetic were commonly taught disciplines. Thus, in Act One, Doalty is learning his seven times table, while Bridget is copying a headline — a line to be written out on her slate. This was the typical way for writing to be taught in hedge-schools, although the headline from Tacitus — 'It's easier to stamp out learning than to recall it' — has not just been chosen for authenticity: it foreshadows the destructive events to come. Maire's work, using the map of America, seems less authentic, but it allows Friel to develop the character by highlighting her desire to emigrate and to embrace modernity.

Pupils' achievements in *Translations* are also commensurate with what we know of real hedge-schools. There are numerous examples of high levels of educational attainment in hedge-schools. The surprise that some audiences feel when they see the juxtaposition of cultural wealth and material poverty was also expressed by Lord Palmerston in County Sligo, who noted the 'miserable mud hut on the road side', where, 'from the appearance of the establishment, no-one would imagine, Latin and even Greek' (Dowling, 1968, p. 37) being taught. Dowling reports an account of 'good Latin scholars who did not understand the English tongue; particularly one Peter Kelly, who lived in a very uncultivated part of the country' (Dowling, 1968, p. 39). This, of course, is reminiscent of Friel's Jimmy Jack Cassie. In the early nineteenth century, however, English was fast supplanting Irish in many hedge-schools as the language in which lessons were taught. Even in remote areas, such as the mountains of Kerry, there were such schools. Dowling reports that the 'hedge schoolmaster was often proud of his English' (Dowling, 1968, p. 59). While many people spoke both English and Irish fluently, sometimes each language was used in a separate context. Dowling cites the example that, in West Cork, Irish was spoken in the fields and the home, while English was used for business. This reminds us of Hugh's disparaging remarks about the English language in Act Two, scene one of *Translations*.

Several of the qualities of individual hedge-school masters can be recognised in Friel's characterisation of Hugh. One headmaster of a hedge-school, Frank Glass, was said to exhibit 'a strange combination of cunning, thought and humour' and 'his love for classical literature amounted to a passion'. Also he 'delighted in Horace' and was celebrated for his 'quaint renderings of the Odes' (Dowling, 1968, p. 41). This might remind us of Hugh's recitation in Act Two, scene one, after which he tells Yolland that 'I dabble in verse…after the style of Ovid.' Also reminiscent of Hugh are some of the characteristics that Dowling cites as being typical of the hedge-school master, including 'his ability to teach… his wit' and his 'knowledge' as well as his 'fondness for displaying his own knowledge' (Dowling, 1968, p. 51). Such qualities are echoed by an account from Thomas Crofton Croker, the antiquary and expert on Irish folklore, who describes the schoolmaster as holding the most distinguished place in any gathering of village statesmen, earned by his historical knowledge, his classical learning and his 'pompous eloquence' (Dowling, 1968, p. 93). Dowling also notes some of the schoolmaster's invaluable 'weapons', such as his 'ready tongue and quick wit' (Dowling, 1968, p. 51). Friel shows Hugh brandishing such weapons on occasions such as his outwitting of Doalty in Act One.

As well as being a colourful character, a hedge-school master enjoyed a high social standing in his community. The schoolmaster was regarded as a 'friend whose counsel was to be sought in all circumstances of stress and difficulty, and whose decisions in important matters carried weight', and who would attend important community events: 'No function of consequence, wedding, christening, or harvest-home took place at which he was not a prominent figure' (Dowling, 1968, p. 89).

Such importance was not only confined to a schoolmaster's pupils and his local area. Dowling writes that a schoolmaster's 'reputation among the body of teachers and among the people generally was almost national' (Dowling, 1968, p. 80). While Hugh's remark to Yolland of Wordsworth — 'did he speak of me to you?' — might be a joke, it might also suggest that Hugh does have a widespread reputation. In addition to being celebrated for teaching, some hedge-school masters were acclaimed poets. Dowling notes that while 'few of the great body of schoolmasters were poets', almost every Irish poet of the '18th and 19th centuries appears to have been a schoolmaster'. In addition, some schoolmasters were authors of important grammars and textbooks. Patrick Lynch, who was taught in hedge-schools and went on to run his own school in Dublin, was also a noted writer. His first important publication was *The Pentaglot Preceptor: or Elementary Institutes of the English, Latin, Greek, Hebrew, and Irish Languages, Vol. I., containing a complete Grammar of the English Tongue. For the Use of schools, and peculiarly calculated for the Instruction of such Ladies and Gentlemen, as may wish to learn without the help of a Master*. The title bears a striking resemblance to that of the book that Hugh mentions he is writing in Act Two. Ironically, Hugh's book often gains a laugh in the theatre, owing to its implausibly long and pompous-sounding title, which is actually shorter than the real thing. The real *Pentaglot Preceptor* was a great

Context

Two of J. P. Dowling's sources note that the love of alcohol was a characteristic trait of the hedge-school master. One writer of 'anti-Irish views' comments that the schoolmaster 'completes his character by adding inebriety to his other accomplishments'. A 'clergyman' also comments that 'the capability of drinking whiskey' (Dowling, 1968, p. 91) is an important qualification for a hedge-school master.

success and named 'teachers, scholars of repute, university professors, Catholic and Protestant clergymen' in its list of subscribers (Dowling, 1968, p. 117).

While the audience might appreciate some aspects of the schoolmaster's importance through the presentation of Hugh, there is also a strong sense that his prestige and the future of his school are being challenged. This is obvious not just in major events such as the coming of the new national school and the changing of the place-names, but also in smaller details such as the derogatory remarks made about Hugh and Manus by Biddy Hanna in her letter. Indeed, this seems in keeping with perhaps the play's major concern: the dying of the Irish language and culture. Friel does not present the audience with a picture of a hedge-school (which we might think to be emblematic of Irish culture) in its heyday; he presents us with a picture of a hedge-school in a state of demise. He is precise about when the action of the play takes place: 1833. This was four years after hedge-schools became legal. The hedge-school of Hugh Mor O'Donnell, therefore, is one that is carrying on after its need has passed: systematic education was beginning to be provided elsewhere for free. Indeed, Hugh might be seen to stand at a crossroads: one path leads to a new life with the new place-names and the new language; the other, down which Jimmy appears to be travelling, leads only to memories of the past, delusions and decay. Dowling tells of James Nash, a lovable schoolmaster who 'died in utter poverty companionless, and nameless' and notes that Nash 'had continued to teach long after the National System of Education had been established and had made almost next to impossible the existence of independent rural schools' (Dowling, 1968, p. 97).

> Friel…presents us with a picture of a hedge-school in a state of demise…carrying on after its need has passed

National schools

In 1831 a Board of Commissioners for National Education was established. This body, comprised of representatives from both Catholic and Protestant churches, aimed to establish a national system of elementary (primary) education for both Catholics and Protestants. It was intended to supersede both the existing Protestant-run schools and the less supervised and more sporadic provision from hedge-schools. The commissioners set up the curriculum and the inspection regime as well as publishing the textbooks. Instruction was carried out through the medium of English. Although the shift in the status of the languages had already been occurring, the establishing of the national schools accelerated this trend. The historian J. C. Beckett notes that as well as doing 'a great deal towards abolishing illiteracy', the new education system did much to hasten the Irish language's demise. Fifty years after the national schools were founded, the Irish-speaking population 'had shrunk into insignificance' (Beckett, 1981, p. 313).

The Ordnance Survey (1824–41)

Established in 1791, the Ordnance Survey was tasked to map Britain accurately in response to fears of invasion from France. By 1824, however, the needs of the survey were civil rather than military. Indeed, much of what Lancey says of the enterprise in Act One of *Translations* is historically accurate: the mapping was in response to the need to address inequities in taxation; it was the first such survey to take place in either Great Britain or Ireland; and the cartography was to be completed in unprecedented detail — to a scale of 6 inches to a mile. Officially known as the Townland Survey of Ireland, the project meant that, for a time, Dublin 'was at the cutting edge of cartographic innovation' (Connolly, 2007, p. 436). It involved 2,000 staff, and, while the work was supervised by the officers of the Royal Engineers and the Royal Artillery, under the command of Colonel Thomas Colby, much of the specialist work was entrusted to highly skilled Irish scholars and historians such as John O'Donovan. Like Yolland in *Translations*, O'Donovan was employed as an orthographer (someone responsible for the correct spelling of place-names), but unlike Yolland, who seems to have drifted into the job (which is carried out mostly by Owen), O'Donovan was one of the finest scholars of Irish of his day.

The survey was carried out on a county-by-county basis, beginning with Derry. It recorded details of aspects such as geology, antiquities and place-names, although not all this information appeared on the maps. The work of the survey was completed just before the Great Famine and the maps 'show the Irish landscape as it approached its population climax, detailing every road and house, field and settlement, in a finely engraved topographical portrait that is austerely beautiful' (Connolly, 2007, p. 436).

The Great Famine (1841–49)

The potato was the staple diet of about a third of the Irish population. A new fungal disease, commonly known as potato blight, caused crop failures in three out of four seasons. The consequences were widespread: high mortality caused by famine and disease, increased emigration and the decline of the cottier class — those who received a small dwelling and plot of land from a farmer, where they grew the potatoes on which

---

Context

Friel notes in the 'Sporadic Diary' that he kept while working on *Translations* that two of the four texts to which he kept returning were a memoir by Colonel Thomas Colby and an edition of the letters of John O'Donovan. The others were J. H. Andrews's *A Paper Landscape*, 1975 (a book about the Ordnance Survey in nineteenth-century Ireland) and J. P. Dowling's *The Hedge-Schools of Ireland*.

Task 13

Write about the extent to which you feel criticisms of the historical accuracy of the Ordnance Survey in *Translations* are valid. Does it matter to your reading of the play that the real survey had no military powers?

their family subsisted. The Great Famine caused, it is estimated, the deaths of around 1 million people.

Anglo-Irish relations were also affected deeply. Many believed that the British did little to alleviate Irish misery, and a deep-seated hatred of the English was one lasting result. In all, many historians view the Great Famine as a watershed in Irish history. Summarising this view, Foster says it 'opened an abyss that swallowed up many hundreds of thousands of impoverished Irish people' (R. F. Foster, *Modern Ireland 1600–1972*, 1989, p. 318). He goes on to point out, however, some of the less widely recognised factors that were at work even before the famine: Ireland, while being dependent on agriculture, was reliant in many cases on outdated and unproductive working methods and had lost significant numbers of young and enterprising workers through emigration. It is also interesting to note that famine was not an isolated occurrence; between 1816 and 1842 there had been 14 significant crop failures.

Task **14**

Remind yourself of Maire's 'sweet smell' speech in Act One.

In what ways might the above historical details shape your response?

To what extent would you expect an Irish audience to feel sympathetic towards her character?

Social and political contexts

While *Translations* is set in an Ireland that was a single country, albeit one that was subject to British rule, the play was conceived and first performed in Northern Ireland, a country with its own complex political and cultural allegiances.

The struggle for independence

From the 1870s onwards there were many political campaigns for separateness from Britain, known as Home Rule. Home Rule was largely a constitutional movement, but revolutionary groups, such as the Irish Revolutionary Brotherhood (IRB) and the Irish Volunteers, were prepared to effect political change through violence. While Britain was at war with Germany in 1916, a group from the IRB, led by Patrick Pearse, combined with Irish Volunteers and men from the Irish Citizen Army to mount an insurrection that was to become known as the Easter Rising. They gained control of the General Post Office in Dublin and read a proclamation of independence. While the fighting only lasted for three days before the rebels surrendered and the uprising did not initially have widespread public support, the response from the British — who executed fifteen leaders and imposed martial law — led to public contempt for British rule and support for the rebels.

In the aftermath of the rising, the rebels continued to prepare for military action, and a group comprised mainly of former Irish Volunteers, known as the Irish Republican Army, mounted campaigns against the British forces from 1919 until 1921. In 1921 the Anglo-Irish Treaty established the Irish Free State as a self-governing country, which would remain in the British Commonwealth. Independence from Britain was not to extend to the whole of the island, however. High percentages of people in the province of Ulster, in the north of the country, were opposed to any form of Home Rule and remained loyal to the union with Britain. When the treaty was signed, a Boundary Commission was set up to determine the boundary of the separate province that would not be part of the Free State, but would remain in the union with Great Britain. Michael Collins, one of the IRA signatories of the treaty, felt that the principle of adhering closely to the wishes of the people would mean that significant areas of Ulster — notably County Fermanagh, County Tyrone and Derry city — would become part of the Free State. These areas, despite having high numbers of Catholics, became part of the province of Northern Ireland, but three counties — Cavan, Monaghan and Donegal — remained with the Free State.

Rather than being a final and acceptable compromise, partition (the breaking up of Ireland into two parts) was the start of a new cycle of violence, which began with the assassination of Michael Collins and a Civil War between pro- and anti-treaty Republicans. Even after the Free State had been accepted by most of the population, the Provisional IRA mounted terrorist campaigns (beginning in 1969) in an attempt to reunite the country by force.

The Northern Ireland conflict

Northern Ireland, with its Unionist majority and its Nationalist minority, was a divided society whose divisions became progressively pronounced. By the late 1960s, discrimination and social separation were prominent features of Northern Irish life: proportionally fewer Catholics were lecturers, lawyers or doctors; Catholics made up only 22% of the student population at the Queen's University of Belfast; discrimination in housing was said to be startlingly high. In addition, as Northern Ireland expanded, the benefits seemed to be given overwhelmingly to Protestants. A new town to be named 'Craigavon' was to be built in a Protestant area; the New University of Ulster was to be situated not in the Catholic city of Derry, but in a small Protestant town called Coleraine.

Context

Nationalists want a united Ireland, in which Northern Ireland becomes part of the independent Republic of Ireland.

Republicans want a united Ireland, but support, or will accept, violence as a means to this.

Unionists wish to maintain independence from the Republic of Ireland and stay as part of the United Kingdom.

Loyalists back the union, but support, or will accept, violence as a means of retaining it.

Taking it *Further*

Why not watch one of these films to give you a sense of some of the Irish struggle for independence?

- *Michael Collins* (1996) is a biopic of the pro-treaty leader and stars the first man to play the role of Doalty, Liam Neeson.
- *The Wind that Shakes the Barley* (2006) depicts the events of the 1920s from the more local perspective of two brothers who join the fight against the British.

Pause for Thought ❚❚

Friel was a member of the Nationalist Party and in 1964 said 'I'm a Nationalist too, you know. I feel very emotionally about this country. I wouldn't attempt to rationalise my feelings, but I get myself involved in stupid controversies about the border' (Delaney, 2000, p. 21).

To what extent does knowing Friel's political views alter your judgement of his play?

Task 15

Write about the ways in which different characters — for example, Manus, Maire, Doalty, Owen, Hugh, the Donnelly twins — react to the British soldiers and how attitudes to them develop during the course of the play. In what ways might each character represent a political viewpoint towards the British in Northern Ireland?

One pressure group, the Northern Ireland Civil Rights Association, protested against injustices against Catholics, and a march against unfair allocation of housing in Derry resulted in violence between protesters and the police. A Protestant backlash against the protesters followed and, in August 1969, the British Army was deployed to keep the peace. Initially welcomed by the Catholics they had come to protect, the soldiers came to be seen as a symbol of oppressive British rule. Violence escalated and in August 1971 the government introduced internment (detention without trial). Hostilities increased: in 1970 there were 25 deaths; in 1971 there were 173; in 1972 there were 467. Support for the IRA increased, and the terrorists took on the role of 'defenders' of Catholic housing estates. In urban areas, such as Belfast and Derry, people living in Catholic and Protestant areas began to separate themselves by erecting barricades between the communities. Some Catholic areas became 'no-go' zones for non-Catholics and the security forces; graffiti on one gable wall read 'You Are Now Entering Free Derry'.

The paramilitaries who 'defended' their — mostly working-class — areas enforced discipline. For example, the typical punishment for a Catholic woman who dated a British soldier would be to suffer ritual humiliation by having her head shaven, then being covered in tar and feathers. After this she would often be tied to a railing in a public place as a warning to other Catholic women.

On 30 January 1972, a banned Civil Rights march in Derry became known as 'Bloody Sunday' after soldiers of the Parachute Regiment were sent to make arrests and shot 13 unarmed civilians (who the soldiers claimed they thought were opening fire on them). Further violence ensued, from both Protestant paramilitary gangs and IRA bombs. On 24 March, the Northern Irish parliament was suspended and the province became governed by direct rule from London.

Attempts to stabilise Northern Ireland by allowing the Republic of Ireland (as the Irish Free State became in 1949) to have some say in its affairs were made by the Sunningdale Agreement of 1973, but this settlement was met with Protestant hostility and a general strike that brought the province to a standstill. Paramilitary violence continued; Catholic complaints about discrimination continued.

While the action of *Translations* takes place in Donegal in 1833, many have seen parallels between the coming of the Royal Engineers with their Ordnance Survey and the coming of British troops to the streets of Northern Ireland.

Education in Northern Ireland

Sectarian divisions were — and, to a large extent, still are — augmented structurally by the education system in Northern Ireland. The non-denominational schools (those without religious affiliation) that were established by the Northern Ireland Education Act of 1923 were boycotted by Catholics and opposed by many Protestants. In Northern Ireland, 'mixed' education does not denote the simultaneous teaching of boys and girls, but the simultaneous teaching of Catholics and Protestants. Even today, few schools in Northern Ireland offer a truly 'mixed' education.

Cultural context

The Irish language

The Free State government wanted Ireland to have a distinct, 'Gaelic' identity. A central part of this was the aspiration to revive the Irish language; in 1911 only 17.6% of the population were able to speak any Irish. Accordingly, Irish became a compulsory subject in the secondary school examinations that were set up in 1929 and proficiency in Irish was (and still is) a prerequisite for most public sector jobs. The policy of reviving the language was largely unsuccessful, however, and today only around 4% of the population use Irish frequently or intensively.

In Northern Ireland there were pockets of success for the language. Some Catholics learnt it as a means of expressing their Irish identity, and in areas like Derry the number of those with some proficiency in the language was proportionally high. It was also used by IRA inmates as a means of more private communication in prison, and many Protestants in Northern Ireland came to view the language with suspicion, associating it with Republicanism. For example, in the late 1980s and early 1990s, in the Students' Union building of Queen's University prominent signs written in the Irish language, with much smaller English translations, were displayed. This caused controversy and led to complaints from some students from Protestant backgrounds.

The Field Day Theatre Company

Founded in 1980 in the embattled city of Derry (or Londonderry), the Field Day Theatre Company was formed by Friel and the Belfast-

Taking it Further

Compare the presentation of anti-Irish discrimination in *Translations* with Roddy Doyle's comic take on this in his 1987 novel *The Commitments*. His protagonist, Jimmy Rabbitte, who forms a soul band, remarks that 'the Irish are the blacks of Europe', then uses this sense of being downtrodden to galvanise his musicians by making them repeat the following words from James Brown's song: 'Say it loud — I'm black and I'm proud!'

born actor Stephen Rea. Its immediate aim was to put on, and tour with, *Translations*, but there was also an intention to make a cultural contribution to a society riven with political unrest. The critic Elmer Andrews recounts that in the first edition of the periodical *Crane Bag*, two critics, Richard Kearney and Mark Hederman, noted that the Irish word for 'province' was also the word for a fifth, and put forward the idea of a fifth province in Ireland — a province outside of the four geographical provinces, a province of the mind. Here, each person could exist in a neutral realm, outside of the myths of the other four: the fifth province would be somewhere 'where all oppositions were resolved' (Andrews, 1995, p. 165).

Central to the conception of Field Day was Derry, the city that would host the premiere of *Translations*. By this stage it had seen Bloody Sunday and numerous Civil Rights marches; it was governed by a Protestant mayoral system, and it contained the highest concentration of the unemployed in western Europe (most of whom were Catholic). On a social and cultural level it had lost out by the decision to situate the country's new university in the Protestant town of Coleraine, rather than Derry, the province's second city (which already had a campus ripe for upgrading in Magee College).

The place in which the play would be performed was not without significance: the Guildhall (which houses the mayor's chambers and which many saw as a symbol of Protestant rule). On 22 September a full house in the Guildhall witnessed the inaugural performance of *Translations*. It was a triumph. Marlene Jefferson, the Unionist mayor of Derry led the ovation, standing beside Eamonn McCann, a Sinn Fein (Republican) activist and John Hume, a Nationalist MP. Its success was repeated on a tour of venues in both the North and South of the country.

Field Day took on a more varied role after *Translations*. The momentum gained by the play's success meant that Seamus Heaney and others urged Friel to continue with Field Day. He responded by inviting them to join the project. A board of directors was formed that also comprised Heaney, poets and lecturers Tom Paulin and Seamus Deane, and the musician David Hammond. In addition to creative work, Field Day began to publish pamphlets on matters such as the Irish language, the relationship between culture and politics and postcolonial readings of the Northern Ireland conflict. Its most ambitious publication was *The Field Day Anthology of Irish Writing* (1991), a huge, three-volume work, which Seamus Deane hoped would help to show the coherence and continuity of Irish literature and provide a vision of the island's 'cultural integrity which would operate as a basis for an enduring and enriching political settlement' (Andrews, 1995, p. 165). The critics received the *Anthology* rather differently. As well as there being an outcry about the work's under-representation of women, many objected to its perceived Nationalist agenda.

Rather than seeing the sense of fun in 'having a field day' or appreciating the phonological playfulness of the blend in the name (Field sounds similar to Friel; Day to Rae), critics of the project were seeing the soldierly connotation of a field day as a time for army training (with the *Anthology*'s militaristically titled 'General Editor', Seamus Deane, presumably assuming command). Some viewed it in Marxist terms, seeing Field Day as a kind of a nationalist 'hegemony' — a self-perpetuating system — that was now controlling the means of cultural production, distribution and interpretation.

It is interesting that with increased Field Day activity, interpretations of *Translations* became increasingly hostile. In 1985, Edna Longley read the play almost as an allegory for perceived British oppression in Northern Ireland: 'When Friel's soldier-researchers deploy unhistorical bayonets after Lieutenant Yolland goes missing, his subject is the behaviour of British troops in the Catholic ghettoes of Belfast and Derry during the 1970s' (E. Longley, *Poetry in the Wars*, 1986, p. 190). Sean Connolly summarised what he saw as historical misrepresentation by writing that the play presents 'an artificial contrast between the hopelessly idealised and the hopelessly debased' (in Andrews, 1995, p. 167).

As early as 1983, Friel feared that his involvement with Field Day could lead to a conflict between his individual work and the needs of the company. Indeed, he noted that it might involve a 'suppression of the personality' (Delaney, 2000, p. 190), and, after *Making History* (1988), he used other companies to produce his plays. In 1994 he formally resigned as a Field Day director.

Literary context

Irish drama

Representations of rural peasant life had already been seen on stage, notably in the plays of W. B. Yeats (1865–1939) and J. M. Synge (1871–1909). While Yeats's plays are known for their use of symbolism, ritual and music, many of Synge's are celebrated for their use of situations

drawn from life in the Aaran islands and their use of authentic-sounding Hiberno-English speech. As Friel would do later in *Translations*, Synge brought realism, humour and wit to his use of dialogue, as well as a skilful blending of tragedy and comedy.

In the hands of later and lesser playwrights, portrayals of situations and characters in Irish settings became clichéd and the 'stage Irishman', whose main purpose was to entertain English audiences, arose.

Northern Irish writing in the 1970s

The poet Seamus Heaney wrote about events in Northern Ireland in ways that have some similarities with those of Friel in *Translations*. For example, in *Wintering Out*, published in 1972, the year of 'Bloody Sunday', Heaney drew on the Irish tradition of *dinnseanchas* — the ancient form that explores the legend embedded in the place-name. While such poems are poetic pronunciations of place-names, they express a reverence for the Irish landscape to which the speaker feels a strong sense of belonging: 'Anahorish' is 'My "place of clear water"'. Yet such closeness to the landscape is under threat: in 'Broagh' the opposition between natives and 'strangers' is confrontational.

Heaney also confronts the conflict in his 1975 collection *North*, several poems from which use imagery inspired by the discovery of bodies preserved in peat bogs in Denmark. In 'Punishment' the subject is, on one level, an Iron Age woman who has been executed for adultery. On another, she is a Northern Irish Catholic who has been tarred and feathered by those in her own community as a punishment for her relationship with a British soldier. In the last stanzas of the poem, the speaker considers his own response: paradoxically, he has given the victim no assistance, yet feels 'civilised outrage' at what has been done to her; but, at the same time, he understands the wider community and its need for 'tribal, intimate revenge'.

Working with the text

Meeting the Assessment Objectives

The four key English Literature Assessment Objectives (AOs) describe the different skills you need to show in order to get a good grade. Regardless of what texts or what examination specification you are following, the AOs lie at the heart of your study of English literature at AS and A2; they let you know exactly what the examiners are looking for and provide a helpful framework for your literary studies.

The Assessment Objectives require you to:

- articulate creative, informed and relevant responses to literary texts, using appropriate terminology and concepts, and coherent, accurate written expression **(AO1)**
- demonstrate detailed critical understanding in analysing the ways in which structure, form and language shape meanings in literary texts **(AO2)**
- explore connections and comparisons between different literary texts, informed by interpretations of other readers **(AO3)**
- demonstrate understanding of the significance and influence of the contexts in which literary texts are written and understood **(AO4)**

Try to bear in mind that the AOs are there to support rather than restrict you; don't look at them as encouraging a tick-box approach or a mechanistic, reductive way into the study of literature. Examination questions are written with the AOs in mind, so if you answer them clearly and carefully, you should automatically hit the right targets. If you are devising your own questions for coursework, seek the help of your teacher to ensure that your essay title is carefully worded to liberate the required assessment objectives so that you can do your best.

Although the Assessment Objectives are common to all the exam boards, the specifications vary enormously in the way they meet

the requirements. The boards' websites provide useful information, including sections for students, past papers, sample papers and mark schemes.

AQA: **www.aqa.org.uk**   EDEXCEL: **www.edexcel.com**

Cambridge International: **www.cie.org.uk**   OCR: **www.ocr.org.uk**

CCEA: **www.rewardinglearning.org.uk**   WJEC: **www.wjec.co.uk**

Remember, though, that your knowledge and understanding of the text still lie at the heart of A-level study, as they always have done. While what constitutes a text may vary according to the specification you are following (e.g. it could be an article, extract, letter, diary, critical essay, review, novel, play or poem), and there may be an emphasis on the different ways in which texts can be interpreted and considered in relation to different contexts, in the end the study of literature starts with, and comes back to, your engagement with the text itself.

Working with AO1

AO1 focuses upon literary and critical insight, organisation of material and clarity of written communication. Examiners are looking for accurate spelling and grammar and clarity of thought and expression, so say what you want to say, and say it as clearly as you can. Aim for cohesion; your ideas should be presented coherently with an overall sense of a developing argument. Think carefully about your introduction, because your opening paragraph not only sets the agenda for your response but provides the reader with a strong first impression of you — positive or negative.

Try to use 'appropriate terminology' but don't hide behind fancy critical terms or complicated language you don't fully understand; 'feature spotting' and merely listing literary terms is a classic banana skin with which all examiners are familiar.

Choose your references carefully; copying out great gobbets of a text learned by heart underlines your inability to select the choicest short quotation with which to clinch your argument. Regurgitating chunks of material printed on the examination paper without detailed critical analysis is — for obvious reasons — a reductive exercise; instead try to incorporate brief quotations into your own sentences, weaving them in seamlessly to illustrate your points and develop your argument.

The hallmarks of a well-written essay — whether for coursework or in an exam — include a clear and coherent introduction that orientates the reader, a systematic and logical argument, aptly chosen and neatly embedded quotations and a conclusion which consolidates your case.

Working with AO2

In studying a text, you should think about its overall form (novel, sonnet, tragedy, farce etc.), structure (how it is organised, how its constituent parts connect with each other) and language. In studying a long novel or a play, it might be better to begin with the larger elements of form and structure before considering language, whereas for a poem, analysing aspects of its language (imagery, for example) might be a more appropriate place to start. If 'form is meaning', what are the implications of your chosen writer's decision to select this specific genre? In terms of structure, why does the on-stage action of one play unfold in real time while another spans months or years? In terms of language features, what is most striking about the diction of your text — dialogue, dialect, imagery or symbolism?

In order to discuss language in detail, you will need to quote from the text — but the mere act of quoting is not enough to meet AO2. What is important is what you do with the quotation — how you analyse it and how it illuminates your argument. Moreover, since you will often need to make points about larger generic and organisational features of your chosen text, such as books, chapters, verses, cantos, acts or scenes which are usually much too long to quote, being able to reference effectively is just as important as mastering the art of the embedded quotation.

Working with AO3

AO3 is a double assessment objective which asks you to 'explore connections and comparisons' between texts as well as showing your understanding of the views and interpretations of others. You will find it easier to make comparisons and connections between texts (of any kind) if you try to balance them as you write; remember also that connections and comparisons are not only about finding similarities — differences are just as interesting. Above all, consider how the comparison illuminates each text. It's not just a matter of finding the relationships and connections, but of analysing what they show. When writing comparatively, use words and constructions that will help you to link your texts, such as: whereas, on the other hand, while, in contrast, by comparison, as in, differently, similarly, comparably.

To access the second half of AO3 effectively, you need to measure your own interpretation of a text against those of your teacher and other students. By all means refer to named critics and quote from them if it seems appropriate, but the examiners are most interested in your personal and creative response. If your teacher takes a particular critical line, be prepared to challenge and question it; there is nothing more dispiriting for an examiner than to read a set of scripts from one centre which all say exactly the same thing. Top candidates produce fresh personal responses rather than merely regurgitating the ideas of others, however famous or insightful their interpretations may be.

Of course, your interpretation will be convincing only if it is supported by clear reference to the text, and you will be able to evaluate other readers' ideas only if you test them against the evidence of the text itself. Achieving AO3 means more than quoting someone else's point of view and saying you agree, although it can be very helpful to use critical views if they push forward an argument of your own and you can offer relevant textual support. Look for other ways of reading texts — from a Marxist, feminist, new historicist, post-structuralist, psychoanalytic, dominant or oppositional point of view — which are more creative and original than merely copying out the ideas of just one person. Try to show an awareness of multiple readings with regard to your chosen text and an understanding that the meaning of a text is dependent as much upon what the reader brings to it as what the writer left there. Using modal verb phrases such as 'may be seen as', 'might be interpreted as' or 'could be represented as' implies that you are aware that different readers interpret texts in different ways at different times. The key word here is plurality; there is no single meaning, no right answer, and you need to evaluate a range of other ways of making textual meanings as you work towards your own.

Working with AO4

AO4, with its emphasis on the 'significance and influence' of the 'contexts in which literary texts are written and received', might at first seem less deeply rooted in the text itself, but in fact you are considering and evaluating here the relationship between the text and its contexts. Note the word 'received': this refers to the way interpretation can be influenced by the specific contexts within which the reader is operating; when you are studying a text written many years ago, there is often an immense gulf between its original contemporary context of production and the twenty-first century context in which you receive it.

To access AO4 successfully you need to think about how contexts of production, reception, literature, culture, biography, geography, society, history, genre and intertextuality can affect texts. Place the text at the heart of the web of contextual factors which you feel have had the most impact upon it; examiners want to see a sense of contextual alertness woven seamlessly into the fabric of your essay, rather than a clumsy bolted-on rehash of a website or your old history notes. Try to convey your awareness of the fact that literary works contain embedded and encoded representations of the cultural, moral, religious, racial and political values of the society from which they emerged, and that over time attitudes and ideas change until the views they reflect are no longer widely shared. And you're right to think that there must be an overlap between a focus on interpretations (AO3) and a focus on contexts, so don't worry about pigeonholing the AOs here.

Essay writing

Traditional coursework tasks

Wider reading is important at A-level and you may need to compare and contrast *Translations* with another text or texts you have studied. Sometimes this text will be set for you by your exam board, or chosen by your teacher, and sometimes the choice of comparative text(s) will be up to you. Clearly you will need to compare and contrast your chosen texts effectively, but beyond this you need to check the appropriate weightings for the relevant AOs as laid down by your particular exam board. AO1 will be assessed throughout your essay, but you should plan carefully to ensure that you spend a proportionate amount of time and effort addressing the specific weightings and requirements of the other AOs.

As well as ensuring that your title clearly addresses the relevant Assessment Objectives and allows for adequate, focused treatment within the word limit, there are a number of crucial stages in the coursework writing process:

- Discuss your proposed title with your teacher as soon as possible.
- Set aside an hour to jot down ideas for the essay and convert them into an essay plan. Share this plan with your teacher and make use of any feedback offered.
- Identify any background reading, such as textual criticism, that may be useful to you, gather the books you need, read them and make notes.
- Give yourself a reasonable period to draft the essay, working with your text, your notes and other useful materials around you.

- Keep referring to the title or question to ensure you remain focused on it.
- Allow time for your teacher to read and comment on your draft.
- Redraft and proofread your essay before handing it in and ensure that you have focused on the relevant AOs.
- A bibliography will add to the professionalism of your essay. This should list all the texts you have consulted. Check which format you are required to use and stick to this.

Sample task

Compare the ways in which Friel and Heaney use the past to understand the present. Consider the interpretations of other readers in your response.

Sample A-grade answer

Both writers use the past to help them view present day problems in a broader historical context. While Heaney shows reverence for Irish history and often seems to present it in a partisan fashion, Friel complicates the notion of history, seeing it as just another narrative, and one that is often riddled with contradictions.

Heaney uses place-names to explore the connection that many Irish Nationalists feel for their country. His reverence for place-names is obvious in his 1972 collection *Wintering Out* in poems such as 'Anahorish' and 'Broagh'. 'Anahorish' begins with a translation: 'My "place of clear water"' and, like Yolland in *Translations*, Heaney's speaker takes pleasure from a loving pronunciation; in this case, its sounds conjure idyllic images of the place: '*Anahorish*, soft gradient/ of consonant, vowel-meadow'. While not overtly political, the poem articulates a sense of belonging: the possessive pronoun 'my' proclaiming the speaker's entitlement to this land, and the later images surrounding the 'mound dwellers' suggesting that his affinity reaches back to ancient times. A more confrontational stance is adopted in 'Broagh'. The 'strangers' in this poem cannot pronounce the place-name; they found that 'last/*gh*.../difficult to manage'. 'Strangers' in an Irish literary context often means the English (Yeats for example has a character warn of the stranger coming to the house in his patriotic play *Cathleen Ni Houlihan*); Heaney quibbles on 'manage' — suggesting both their failed attempts to pronounce the place-name and their attempts to control the natives. In both poems the reader is encouraged to identify with the speaker, whose rootedness is reinforced by form, since both are written in the *dinnseanchas* tradition — the ancient Irish form that explores the legend embedded in the place-name.

While Heaney mostly presents Irish experience from one side, Friel's play complicates notions of belonging and acceptance by using an English character, Yolland, to fight to preserve Irish culture. Even though Friel's play ultimately makes the audience sympathise with the Irish and their loss of language and culture, the villains and victims are less easy to define than in Heaney's poems. For example, while 'Broagh' creates an opposition between the natives and the 'strangers', Friel deconstructs the simplistic binarism of English conqueror and Irish victim through the characters Yolland and Owen. This might be suggested in production at the beginning of Act Two when Owen, the civilian employee of British Army, sits '*totally engrossed*' at the map (which symbolises the conquest that he is assisting) while Yolland, the romantic 'soldier by accident' lies with '*his eyes closed*', resting his head against a '*creel*' (which symbolises the simple Irish way of life that he would like to share). While Yolland, like the strangers in 'Broagh', does find it 'difficult to manage' some words — like 'poteen', which he says three times in one line, showing his frustration at being unable to acquire Gaelic quickly — he wants to become part of Irish society, rather than to help to rule it. Yolland can be the best-liked character on stage, and while hatred of Lancey and the British rule that he might be seen as representing forms a large part of the audience's response, this is mitigated by love for Yolland, who shows that we cannot view everybody from a given culture as being the same.

Heaney, however, presents the Irish as a unified people — a people who are often presented as the victims of history. In 'Act of Union' Heaney juxtaposes two sonnets: one is written in the voice of a wronged woman, the other in the voice of the rake who wronged her. This allegory of the forced union between England and Ireland — its title punning with the 1800 Act of Parliament that forcibly yoked Ireland to Britain — inevitably simplifies the complexities of the historical events. The 'imperially/male' personification of England is haughty and shows no love for what will be his bastard offspring, and no respect for its mother, whom he views coldly as just another conquest. The poem ends with imagery that blends language of the landscape and the labour ward: Ireland's 'tracked/And stretchmarked body' will suffer 'big pain' and be 'raw like opened ground again.' The pessimistic message about the England/Ireland relationship is reinforced by the couplet, which rhymes 'pain' and 'again', leaving

the reader with a sense that the victimised country has suffered in the past and will suffer in the future. Some might object to such a reading of Irish history, which casts Ireland as a woman who must passively endure. As well as it being unfavourable from a feminist perspective — a second perpetrator of this act of abuse might be seen to be the male poet who exploits an image of femininity, objectifying her into passivity — it presents the country as having only a single voice, which in this case is mournful and weak.

Friel's play, by contrast, presents a variety of Irish responses to the linguistic and cultural takeover of the 1830s. Passivity is shown in characters like Sarah who retreats into silence, but active rebellion is visible in the response of others. Some might approve of the defiance of simple rural workers like Doalty, who vows 'I've damned little to defend but he'll not put me out without a fight', perhaps even interpreting them as a justification for supporting the IRA. Yet there are other views, such as Hugh's more cryptic responses. His final speech is not always wholly clear as he struggles to remember his Virgil as the lights fade, but the imagery of 'blood' and 'kings proud of war' — especially if there are sound effects of burning or fighting in the background — might make the audience feel he is resigned to the violence ahead. He also, however, voices a degree of acceptance: he promises to teach Maire English and he says that the Irish should 'learn to make [the new place-names] our own. We must make them our new home.' Therefore, rather than seeing the Irish as passive, or aggressive, there is a sense in which they can accept the British conquest, yet through their appropriation of a distinctive form of the English language they can gain something from the experience.

Something is gained in some of Heaney's poems, yet the gains are less tangible. In 'Requiem for the Croppies' Heaney adopts the second person plural perspective to show the solidarity of those who rose up against the British in 1798, but this technique also implies that the rebels were a homogeneous group, which is surely an oversimplification, when we consider that the United Irishmen are often celebrated as a group encompassing both Catholics and Protestants. The sonnet builds to a moment of heroic sacrifice, as those farmers who fought with 'shaking scythes at cannon' fell and 'the hillside blushed, soaked in our broken wave'. It is as if the very landscape is embarrassed that the British could be so cruel, and Heaney concludes on a note of hope as 'in August the barley grew up out of the grave'. The final line is not part of a couplet that presents a neat solution as in so many other sonnets; its rhyme takes the reader back to the twelfth line — 'the blushing hillside' and the 'broken wave' — and thus, rather than claim that any resounding conclusion was reached by the efforts of the croppies, Heaney reminds us of their blood sacrifice. He creates a cyclical effect through his final line, as in the first line the speakers spoke of going into battle with 'The pockets of our greatcoats full of barley.' This crop has now flourished. Given that the poem was written in 1966, when many were commemorating another rising, that of Easter 1916, the poem might be suggesting that the spirit of rebellion and the nobility of sacrifice in the face of British oppression will always continue.

A different view of the 1798 rebellion is advanced by Friel's character, Hugh. Rather than claim an understanding of the whole insurrection, Hugh focuses on the specific feelings of two would-be rebels, himself and Jimmy. But far from being a story of shared heroism, Hugh explores personal feelings of failed patriotism. Friel does not deal with the specifics of action as Heaney did when he commented on 'the tactics' such as the way they'd 'cut through reins and rider with the pike/And stampede cattle into infantry' — Hugh's memories are more subjective as he explains the march as a moment of epiphany, when he felt 'a congruence, a miraculous matching of hope and past and present and possibility', when 'the rhythms of perception heightened' and 'The whole consciousness accelerated'. Unlike Heaney's miraculous ending, Friel uses bathos, ending Hugh and Jimmy's rebellion 'in Phelan's pub'. But the memory goes on to elevate the experience: Hugh dignifies it using Latin terms — such as the '*desiderium nostrorum*' and their '*pietas*' for 'older, quieter things'. But this is not an apologia for cowardice, but a celebration of the stronger claim of loyalty to the family.

Heaney's speakers, by contrast, are clear about their part in history, and the reader is in no doubt where his or her sympathies should lie. Perhaps rather than condemn him for being partisan we should praise him for reflecting his feelings and the feelings of his community with candour, even if — as in 'Punishment' — looking back at his past justifies his tribal present. It might also be unfair to criticise a poem written as a form of 'requiem' for doing exactly what its title suggests: praising and remembering the dead. Throughout, and particularly in his place-name poems, the past helps to communicate a strong sense of belonging. While it is true that Friel presents a more pluralistic view of history, the overwhelming sense of Friel's play is that of loss. Unlike Heaney's poetry, which stresses the continuity of Irish experience, Friel's play makes the audience dwell on the loss of the Irish language, and for that the British

Top ten *quotation* ❯

bear a heavy responsibility. Yet, even if it is possible to find a dominant historical narrative in his play, the way in which he demonstrates that there are no such things as 'the "facts" of history' and leaves the audience with so many unanswered questions means that it is unfair to criticise him as manipulating the past to provide a simple anti-British message. Indeed, unlike Heaney, Friel's version of the past is puzzlingly complex: it is puzzling to recognise that the past is open to interpretations and that any lessons it has are governed as much by the views of the teacher as by the facts themselves. That, I think is Friel's point, and while for Heaney, the past is a source of understanding for the present, for Friel it is a source of confusion which leads to further thought. This we should celebrate. As Hugh, who is thought by many to be the closest character to the views of his creator, says, toasting Jimmy: 'My friend, confusion is not an ignoble condition.'

There are examiner's comments on a different essay with this title as well as further possible essay titles and selected student responses on the Downloads section of the free website which accompanies this book. Go to: **www.philipallan.co.uk/literatureguidesonline**

Transformational writing

Another type of coursework is the transformative option, in which you must show your awareness of genre, context and the intricacies of language through a piece of creative writing. This hands-on approach is certainly not an easier option than the traditional essay, as it requires you to unify creative and critical textual approaches; you must analyse Friel's choices of form, structure and language in detail before attempting to write your own piece. Working with your source text, you may have to create a new scene or speech, retell part of the story from an alternative viewpoint or change the genre altogether, which will mean reading and re-reading the play actively and imaginatively. Your aim should be to produce an original written response, which remains rooted convincingly within the original play.

Sample task

Script a conversation between Manus and Maire that takes place after Act Two, scene two, before the dance. You should aim to build upon Friel's presentation of their characters and capture aspects of his chosen form, structure and language. You should also produce a brief commentary which analyses the particular effects you have tried to create and how these relate to the source text.

Critical debate tasks

Examination questions often invite you to think about a viewpoint and, by implication, go on to debate this. Any frame of words such as 'how far?' or 'to what extent?' implies that a straight 'yes or no' answer will be insufficient — you must consider both sides of the view and construct a coherent argument.

Sample task

How far do you agree with the view that the ending of *Translations* 'lacks dramatic power and disappoints the audience by ending the play in confusion'?

Extract-based (part-to-whole) tasks

Some tasks may require you to look at a specific section of the text in detail and then branch out from this to consider how and why key themes and ideas dealt with here may be reflected elsewhere in the play.

Key questions to ask when attempting any part-to-whole task are:

- Why has Friel included this section and what is its place in the development of the plot?
- What is the function of the given section in the dramatic structure of the play?
- Are there any parallels or contrasts with other episodes? What would the play lose without this section?
- What does this section reveal about the major characters?
- How far does this section develop the play's themes; how far is it typical of the ways in which Friel deals with these ideas elsewhere?
- How far does the section illustrate typical aspects of Friel's form, structure and language?
- What is the ratio or balance of stage directions to dialogue?
- Are theatrical effects, such as music, used to evoke a mood, and if so, how do they work?
- What is going on between the characters present, and what is the impact of any entrances and exits?

Sample task

Remind yourself of Act Two, scene two. What is the importance of this scene in the play as a whole?

Extended commentary

Act Two, scene one, pp. 48–56

From 'Poteen — poteen — poteen' until 'I'll decode you yet.'

Yolland has just been corrected in his pronunciation of the word 'poteen' (pronounced 'pot-cheen', not 'pot-een'). He says the word three times to try to learn it, and the actor playing Yolland might try to convey both his desire to learn and his frustration with the learning process. The difficulty of acquiring the language leads to a deeper frustration as he realises that even if he spoke it, he will never be accepted fully into Irish society and that 'The private core will always be…hermetic'. His words reinforce his outsider status and the impenetrability of Irish society: the inner part is both a 'core' and 'private'; that area is 'hermetic' — both completely sealed and mystical. Recognising this occult, forbidden aspect — which he knows he will never penetrate — makes it more attractive to him.

Top ten _quotation_ >

Yolland's desire to be Irish might be suggested by his costume. Perhaps '_The hot weather_' has enabled him to discard his red jacket, which connotes his role as part of the colonising force. His white shirt might be open-necked to suggest his romantic spirit (the audience will discover in a few moments that he once lived close to Wordsworth), and even his boots might be removed to make his dress more like the rural workers of Baile Beag — in most productions, Doalty and the female characters go barefoot. Also he is probably not looking at Owen, who makes the glib reply that 'You can learn to decode us', but is reclined and musing on his fate to 'always be an outsider'. There is something tragic about Yolland's knowledge: he recognises he will never be accepted, but he seems helpless to do anything but try.

Top ten _quotation_ >

As Hugh enters the mood shifts. '_Yolland leaps respectfully to his feet_' as soon as this custodian of Irish culture comes in. Throughout the exchange that follows, Yolland is presented as being deferential towards Hugh: he compliments his Latin verse, he is eager to tell him he is 'learning to speak Irish' and he continually calls him 'sir'. Like Yolland the audience might also be in awe, if not of Hugh, then of the riches of the Irish language and Irish culture. Friel wrote primarily for an Irish audience, and since few of them actually speak Irish (only around 4% of the population), they might empathise with Yolland's desire to learn. Yet

Friel's presentation of Irish culture, and Hugh in particular, is much more ambiguous than might at first be recognised.

His entrance line of Latin verse is a good example. The poetry is less impressive than amusing. While there were real hedge-school master poets, Hugh's imitation of Ovid is a triumph of sound over sense, although his comment that 'English succeeds in making it sound… plebeian' might be taken as a comic restatement of a key theme — that every act of translation is an act of control that necessitates loss or distortion.

Friel uses bathos to undercut Hugh's pomposity. Following an impressive speech about Irish linguistic riches being the consequence of material poverty, he turns to Owen and asks, 'Can you give me the loan of half-a-crown?' Indeed, recognising that Hugh is like an actor — we remember that 'as the scene progresses, one has the sense that he is deliberately parodying himself' — might make us doubt the truth of his earlier story about the national school. We have heard him exaggerate and seen him posture throughout the play, so might he have exaggerated a job application into a job offer? Yet rather than see him as being a deceitful character, we might view him as a tragic figure: one whose dignity and prestige have been undermined since the first national schools arrived; one who offers a style of education that is growing more and more out of date, and whose attendance at village functions, where once he would have been the most esteemed figure, is now perhaps requested only through a sense of duty.

Yet there is another side to Hugh: as Yolland recognises, he is astute and 'knows what's happening'. While Owen dismisses this, suggesting that Hugh is not 'able to adjust for survival', we know that he is underestimating his father, who, in Act Three, is willing to adjust not only by accepting the loss of the potential job, but also by agreeing to adopt the new names and begin teaching English. Perhaps Owen might be played as someone who is not so much unable to see that 'something is being eroded', but as someone who does not want to admit it. His long sentences which fade into ellipsis sound like the words of someone who is protesting too much, in contrast to Yolland's short declaratives, which put forward his views simply, clearly and convincingly. Owen's shift in tone to becoming more agitated and even aggressive — 'All right! Fine! Fine!' — might give the impression that he is trying to hide something from himself.

Friel varies the pace by giving Owen a large speech about Tobair Vree, the crossroads where Yolland and Maire have their first — and fateful — date, and whose name they are supposed to change. Friel uses the

speech to intensify the conflict between the characters. Owen might speak quickly as he tries to justify the change of name; his questions might be delivered confrontationally as he challenges Yolland to disagree with him, even using one of his words — 'eroded' — to sarcastically refute the Englishman's view.

Yolland does disagree. Using brief, confident statements, he stands up to Owen and refuses to Anglicise 'Tobair Vree'. Drunk on his love of the Irish language as well as poteen, Yolland keeps 'piety with a man long dead, long forgotten, his name "eroded" beyond recognition, whose trivial little story nobody in the parish remembers'. Ironically, this fidelity to language and its roots leads to a reassertion of Irishness in Owen — the character whose identity seems the most fluid. When Yolland insists 'That's what you want, too, Roland', he ignites Owen's anger at being misnamed — something he has tolerated since Act One. He '(*explodes*) George! For God's sake! *My name is not Roland!*' The intensity of the explosion is short-lived; it clears the air, leading to an increased closeness between the Irishman and the 'stranger'. Twice Friel's stage directions tell us that they 'explode' with laughter, their merriment reaching a climax with Owen's coinage of 'Oland!' — a blend of both English and Irish names and identities. This joyful fusion marks the play's most optimistic moment and suggests that there can be an acceptance of plural identities, as well as harmony between the British and the Irish.

Manus's entry and his refusal to speak English 'for the benefit of the colonist' remind us of the precarious nature of agreement in Anglo-Irish affairs. Tobair Vree, the crossroads where we might have imagined the laughter of happy maidens dancing, is crossed with foreboding: its X is not only the promise of Maire's kiss, it also marks the spot where, metaphorically speaking, a time bomb will be detonated; the explosions of laughter will soon revert to explosions of anger, and ultimately become the bombs and bullets which will resound once the final curtain has fallen.

Top ten quotations

1

Sweet smell! Sweet smell! Every year at this time somebody comes back with stories of the sweet smell. Sweet God, did the potatoes ever fail in Baile Beag? Well, did they ever — ever? Never!

(Maire, Act One, p. 18)

This quotation is the beginning of Maire's diatribe against Irish pessimism. Its power grows as Maire repeats 'sweet smell', mocking the idea that people have smelt the potato blight; her sarcasm turns into the venomous profanity — 'Sweet God' — as she questions the villagers directly, and her speech reaches a self-assured mini-climax as she answers her own question with the exclamation, 'Never!' Despite characterising Maire as strong, opinionated and ambitious, the speech is laced with dramatic irony. Twelve years later, the blight did come, which was responsible for the deaths of 1 million people.

Even if I did speak Irish I'd always be an outsider here, wouldn't I? I may learn the password but the language of the tribe will always elude me, won't it? The private core will always be...hermetic, won't it?

2

(Yolland, Act Two, scene one, p. 48)

Implying that there are levels of linguistic accomplishment, Yolland suggests that while a non-native speaker might gain some acceptance, it would be impossible for such a person to be admitted to the heart of Baile Beag society. 'Hermetic' implies that this core is sealed to outsiders and — through the word's origins in the occult disciplines of alchemy and astrology — that, at a deeper level, there is something secret and mystical about language.

You'll find, sir, that certain cultures expend on their vocabularies and syntax energies and ostentations entirely lacking in their material lives. I suppose you could call us a spiritual people.

3

(Hugh, Act Two, scene one, p. 50)

Hugh's pronouncements in Act Two, scene one are ambiguous, and when you analyse them, it is worth remembering Friel's stage direction, *'as the scene progresses, one has the sense that he is deliberately parodying himself'*. The first sentence might at first glance seem to praise the richness of Irish language and literature, yet it could equally acknowledge that deprivation is a salient feature of Irish life. The second sentence might, therefore, be sarcastic: the Irish make a virtue of necessity by being spiritually rich in order to compensate for being materially poor.

Yes, it is a rich language, Lieutenant, full of the mythologies of fantasy and hope and self-deception — a syntax opulent with tomorrows. It is our response to mud

4

cabins and a diet of potatoes; our only method of replying
to...inevitabilities.

(Hugh, Act Two, scene one, p. 51)

Hugh presents the richness of Irish culture as a sham, comprised as
it is of falsehoods. From Hugh and his unrealistic hope of being the
headmaster of the school, to Jimmy's fantasy of marrying a goddess,
to Owen's claims about the harmlessness of the renaming project, one
might argue that self-deception is endemic in Irish life. The mentions of
'mud cabins' and the meagre 'diet of potatoes', by contrast, are starkly
realistic and present Irish culture (in the sense of their way of life) as
being primitive.

5

YOLLAND	**A thousand baptisms! Welcome to Eden!**
OWEN	**Eden's right! We name a thing and — bang! it leaps into existence!**
YOLLAND	**Each name a perfect equation with its roots.**
OWEN	**A perfect congruence with its reality.**

(Act Two, scene one, p. 56)

Here the recently reconciled characters transmit a sense of friendship
and joy. Their closeness is evoked by the ways their speeches
mirror each other. For example, Owen picks up on Yolland's use of
exclamations and the word 'Eden'; the final two speeches have almost
identical syntax. But beneath this harmony lies the falseness of their
words: the naming project is not like the story of Adam naming the
animals in the Genesis chapter of the Christian Bible; they live in a
fallen world, not the Garden of Eden; the naming project will bring
discord, not harmony. In the next scene Yolland's naïve belief in Baile
Beag as a paradise will bring trouble when he tastes the forbidden
fruit of an exogamous relationship.

6

YOLLAND	**Bun na hAbhann?** *(He says the name softly, almost privately, very tentatively, as if he were searching for a sound she might respond to. He tries again.)* **Druim Dubh?** *Maire stops. She is listening. Yolland is encouraged.* **Poll na gCaorach. Lis Maol.** *Maire turns towards him.* **Lis na nGall.**
MAIRE	**Lis na nGradh.** *They are now facing each other and begin moving — almost imperceptibly — towards one another.*

(Act Two, scene two, pp. 65–66)

This quotation marks a major turning point. The audience has been tantalised by the attempts of Maire and Yolland to come together: they started off holding hands, then moved apart; they grew close, then parted again. Different forms of language have been tried and have failed, including using gestures, the elements and Maire's learned English sentence. Now, ironically, what unites them is what the British have begun to destroy: the Irish language. The very Irish names that Yolland has been tasked to change facilitate real communication; the language of places has become the language of love. Friel explores his major theme in a non-naturalistic and non-rational way. Movements on stage and sounds that are largely incomprehensible to the audience demonstrate the value of the Irish language more eloquently than the most convincing verbal argument.

When my grandfather was a boy they did the same thing… (***almost dreamily.***) **I've damned little to defend but he'll not put me out without a fight.**

7

(Doalty, Act Three, pp. 83–84)

Doalty's lines seem to encourage the audience to view the shabby British behaviour towards the Irish in 1833 as representative of their behaviour throughout Irish history. Accordingly, some might view the quotation as a justification for Republicanism. It certainly reinforces parallels between the events on stage and events in contemporary Northern Ireland, and encourages the audience to identify with the Irish, who are no longer the victims that Maire painted them as in Act One, but plucky heroes who are prepared to fight against superior forces to protect their way of life.

We must learn where we live. We must learn to make them our own. We must make them our new home.

8

(Hugh, Act Three, p. 88)

Hugh's words exemplify what linguists call the Sapir–Whorf hypothesis: the theory that language alters perception. Since the names of their homes have been changed, the Irish must relearn where they live. While he voices a dignified acceptance of the inevitable, there is a sense of regeneration in Hugh's final sentence: the Irish might have been forced to use a foreign language, but they will rework that language until it becomes their own and produces some of the greatest works of English literature.

…it is not the literal past, the 'facts' of history, that shape us, but images of the past embodied in language…we must never cease renewing those images; because once we do, we fossilise.

9

(Hugh, Act Three, p. 88)

Hugh articulates one of Friel's ideas about history and language, that, to borrow the words of the Renaissance philosopher Michel de Montaigne, 'we need to interpret interpretations more than to interpret things'. Such a view is pertinent to Northern Ireland, where both Catholic and Protestant communities celebrate versions of their history that shape their viewpoints. Friel seems to counsel against believing too much in such interpretations and warns that to be overly wedded to the past is to stunt progress in the present and future.

10

> **Do you know the Greek word *endogamein*? It means to marry within the tribe. And the word *exogamein* means to marry outside the tribe. And you don't cross those borders casually — both sides get very angry.**
>
> **(Jimmy, Act Three, p. 90)**

This quotation from the final moments of Act Three combines many of the play's motifs. The erudite use of Greek brings to mind the romantic view of the hedge-school as a place in which serious scholars are nurtured; the absurd suggestion of a tramp marrying a goddess is typical of its sense of fun; yet the sinister subtext reminds us of the fatal consequences of ignoring tribal loyalties. While some might claim that Jimmy's words voice Friel's understanding of sectarian violence, this is only one of the many views that he airs in his play.

Taking it further

Criticism

- Andrews, E. (1995) *The Art of Brian Friel*, Macmillan
  - There is an illuminating chapter entitled 'Rewriting History: The Plays of the 1980s' which not only offers insights on *Translations*, but also explores some of the wider contexts involving the Field Day Theatre Company. The chapter also contains an excellent discussion of the complexities of the character Hugh.
- Coult, T. (2003) *About Friel: The Playwright and the Work*, Faber and Faber
  - Includes helpful details on the genesis of *Translations*, quotations from Friel's diary, and extracts from interviews by those who have worked with Friel.

- Daley, T. and Jones, M. (2005) *Education Background Pack: Translations*, National Theatre Education (see 'Websites' below)
  – A resource pack by Tom Daley and Malcolm Jones on the 2005 National Theatre production.
- Delaney, P. (ed.) (2000) *Brian Friel in Conversation*, University of Michigan Press
  – An invaluable source for discovering Friel's views and intentions.
- Dowling, P. J. (1968) *The Hedge Schools of Ireland*, Mercier Press
  – The standard work on hedge-schools, which Friel read and re-read as he wrote *Translations*.
- Grene, N. (1999) *The Politics of Irish Drama*, Cambridge University Press
  – A scholarly, yet accessible study of Irish drama that contains an excellent section on *Translations*.
- Jones, N. (2000) *A Faber Critical Guide: Brian Friel*, Faber and Faber
  – Provides an accessible introduction to Friel and four of his plays including *Translations*.
- Kearney, R. (1988) *Transitions*, Manchester University Press
  – Contains an illuminating chapter on Friel, which considers the nature of translation, drawing on material from George Steiner, whose book *After Babel* was a key influence on *Translations*.
- Kiberd, D. (1996) *Inventing Ireland*, Vintage
  – An impressive and comprehensive study, which is informed by a wide range of critical approaches, but is approachable and written in an engaging style. The stimulating essay on *Translations* considers the play from a variety of perspectives.
- Longley, E. (1986) *Poetry in the Wars*, Vintage
  – Edna Longley's essay 'Poetry and Politics in Northern Ireland' provides insights on the wider social and political contexts of Northern Irish writing; her prose is both combative and witty.
- O'Brien, G. (1989) *Brian Friel*, Gill and Macmillan
  – Provides an accessible and useful study of the play.
- Steiner, G. (1998) *After Babel: Aspects of Language and Translation*, Oxford University Press
  – An academic study of translation and its implications. While quite a demanding read for A-level students, it might be useful to read Chapter One, 'Understanding as Translation', if you are writing on an aspect of language.

History

- Beckett, J. C. (1981) *The Making of Modern Ireland 1603–1923*, Faber and Faber
  - A traditional, chronological history.
- Connolly, S. J. (ed.) (2007) *The Oxford Companion to Irish History*, Oxford University Press
  - Includes informative entries on many relevant issues, such as the Townland Survey of Ireland and some of its key figures, such as John O'Donovan.
- Foster, R. F. (1989) *Modern Ireland 1600–1972*, Penguin
  - Up-to-date, informed by 'revisionist' approaches and with some very useful material on recent Irish history.

Websites

- www.irishtimes.com/indepth/brian-friel/
  - A series of short articles commissioned on Friel's eightieth birthday.
- http://web.ku.edu/~idea/special/playnames/translationsirish.pdf
  - A list of the Irish and English names, terms and idioms used in *Translations*.
- http://web.ku.edu/~idea/special/playnames/translationsirish.mp3
  - A recording of the names in the play with correct pronunciation by Barbara Carswell and Paul Meier.
- www.paulmeier.com/booklets.html.
  - Accent and Dialect booklets and instruction CDs (one for each character) for *Translations* are available from the above site.
- www.nationaltheatre.org.uk/40325/past-productions/resources-to-download.html
  - The resource pack by Tom Daley and Malcolm Jones on the 2005 National Theatre production may be obtained from the above site.
- http://theater.nytimes.com/2007/01/26/theater/reviews/26tran.html
  - *The New York Times* website has details of the production on Broadway in 2007, directed by Garry Hynes. There is a useful slide show with a commentary.